The Forgotten Trail

———

ONE MAN'S
ADVENTURES
ON THE
CANADIAN ROUTE
TO THE
KLONDIKE

The Forgotten Trail

ONE MAN'S ADVENTURES ON THE CANADIAN ROUTE TO THE KLONDIKE

Larry Pynn

Doubleday Canada Limited

Canadian Cataloguing in Publication Data

Pynn, Larry
    The forgotten trail
ISBN 0-385-25535-7

1. Pynn, Larry—Journeys—Yukon Territory. 2. Yukon Territory—Description and travel. 3. Klondike River Valley (Yukon)—Gold discoveries. I. Title.

FC4017.3.P95 1996   917.19'1043 C96-930576-1 F1091.P95 1996

Map by Robbie Voteary
Jacket photographs by Larry Pynn
Jacket design by Andrew Smith
Text design by Heidy Lawrance Associates
Printed and bound in the U.S.A.

Published in Canada by
Doubleday Canada Limited
105 Bond Street
Toronto, Ontario
M5B 1Y3

To my mother, Frances,
and my father, Art.
Pure gold.

Contents

ACKNOWLEDGEMENTS

After twenty years in this business, I continue to be amazed at how easily complete strangers open up their lives to me, share their fears and desires, expose their secret vulnerabilities. For some, ego might play a part. For others, plain naivety about the power of modern communicators. But for the most part, I put it down to this: people have things to say—interesting, important, even enlightened things—but so rarely does anyone take the time to listen. Conversations between two persons inevitably begin with the word "I," each participant in an unstated struggle with the other for dominance. A good journalist can sever that sort of verbal tug-of-war. When one walks up unannounced and asks, sincerely, "Will you tell me your story?", few people are able to resist the opportunity. After all, it may never come again.

To all those people who opened up their lives during the research of *The Forgotten Trail* (names are unnecessary, you'll find them in the following pages), I extend an honest thank you. You have enriched my life, caused me to rethink my own values and contributed to the cultural record of Canada.

There are also others who are not named, but who helped in

their own way, often quietly and behind the scenes, toward the success of this book. Librarians, the unsung heroes of so many books, certainly deserve their share of praise, especially David Mattison of the British Columbia Archives and Jan Turner of the Pacific Press Library. Archibald Rollo, Column One editor at the *Vancouver Sun*, boosted the scope of my research by twice publicizing my exploits. Among the nuggets that surfaced from the ensuing exposure was the previously unpublished diary of the late John Deeks, who followed the Stikine Route in 1898 en route to a successful mining career in Atlin. Deeks's granddaughter, Wendy Lindmeier, and daughter, Dorothy Moore, unselfishly loaned me that priceless document with just a friendly handshake. The memoirs of miner-cum-telegraph lineman Guy Lawrence are published with the approval of Caryall Books Ltd. I am also grateful to my Victoria editor, Janet Craig, for the tireless enthusiasm and professionalism she brought to this project. *Equinox* magazine gave me a valuable kickstart by agreeing at the beginning to publish a feature article on my exploits. Charlene Porsild, an assistant professor of history at Simon Fraser University, allowed me access to her own extensive archival research on the Klondike gold rush. Don Tyerman, a former newspaperman with an uncanny recollection of Vancouver history, served as my mentor, while his daughter, Janie, an excellent photojournalist in her own right, never wavered in her support of my writing. And, finally, a special thanks to everyone, paid or volunteer, involved in search and rescue in Canada. May we never meet again.

FOREWORD

When Larry Pynn undertook to follow the old Stikine Trail to the Yukon, he found it hadn't changed much over the years and, as a knowledgeable wordsmith with a flare for recreating a historic picture of endurance and effort, he recounts just how tough men and women can be when their dreams lead them into the unknown. Larry found the trail is still paved with the ghosts of men and dogs and horses that died along the way. Not much wonder, for the people had no knowledge of what they faced and their animals had no choice.

I've wandered through that country myself over the years and succumbed to the lure of distant horizons as well as the trauma of getting there despite muskegs, bugs and tangled brush. Sometimes what is a most enjoyable, peaceful and warm stretch of wilderness road can be transformed—about as quickly as you can snap your fingers—into a life-threatening explosion of noise and action. Sometimes an accident will spill a person into water that is only a couple of degrees above freezing, where he has no chance unless he is lucky enough to find a way out quickly.

Larry Pynn is a master storyteller, clean and crisp, with no boggy spots in his narrative. He takes the reader with him and he tells with generosity and humour of the people met along the way. This book is much more than just another good read; it is a classic.

Andy Russell

THE STIKINE ROUTE

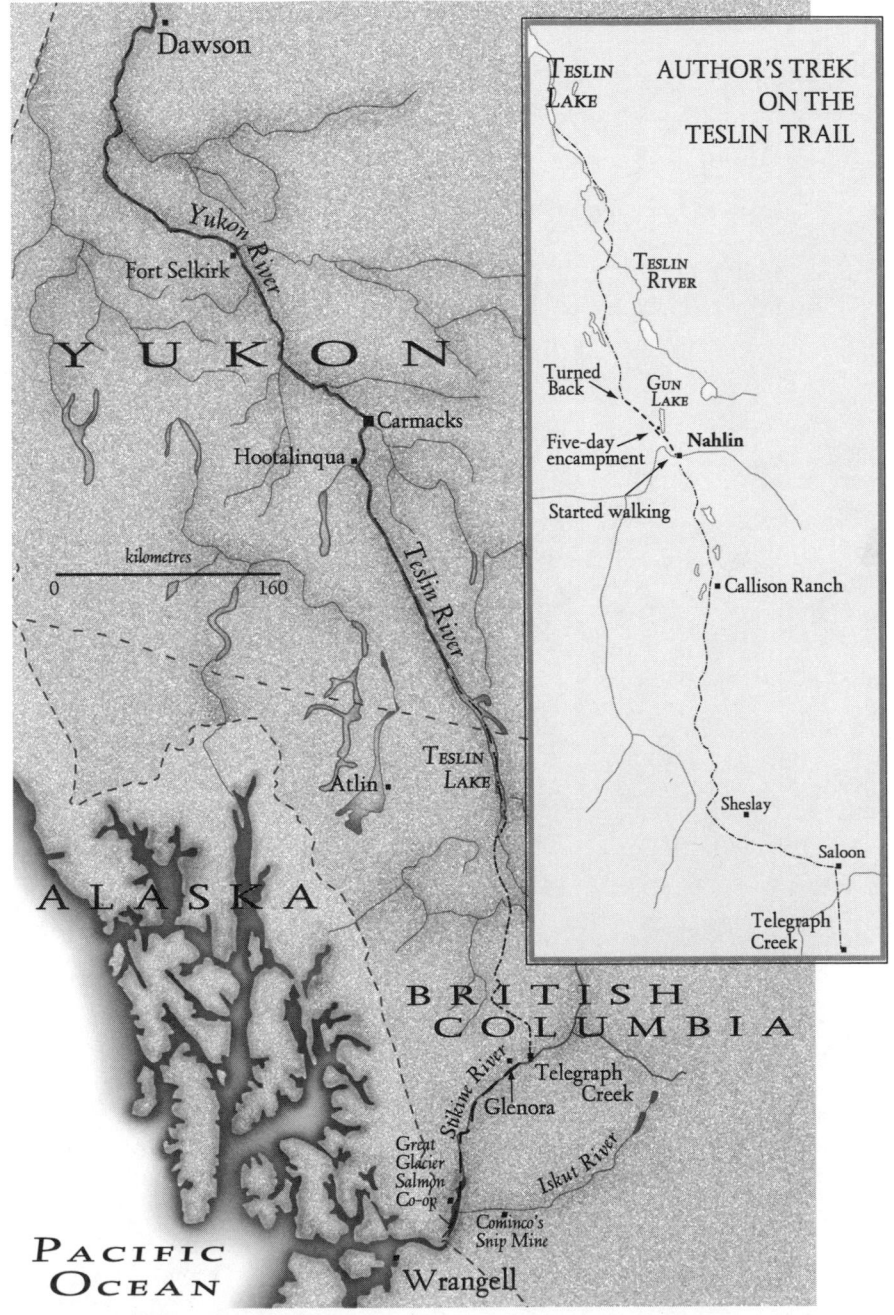

Dawson

Yukon River

Fort Selkirk

Y U K O N

Carmacks

Hootalinqua

Teslin River

kilometres

0   160

Atlin

Teslin Lake

A L A S K A

B R I T I S H
C O L U M B I A

Stikine River

Glenora

Telegraph Creek

Iskut River

Great Glacier Salmon Co-op

Cominco's Snip Mine

Wrangell

PACIFIC OCEAN

AUTHOR'S TREK ON THE TESLIN TRAIL

Teslin Lake

Teslin River

Turned Back

Gun Lake

Five-day encampment

Nahlin

Started walking

Callison Ranch

Sheslay

Saloon

Telegraph Creek

INTRODUCTION

The Klondike. Few Canadian place-names can say so much or engender such deep and passionate emotions. Indeed, throughout the world there is no single incident in Canadian history that is better known than the Klondike stampede, that crazed, headlong dash a century ago to the goldfields of Dawson City, Yukon. To some it speaks of romance, to others of high adventure. Whatever our views of the Klondike gold rush—and however far those views may be from the harsh reality—there is no denying the enduring legacy of this brief, frenzied event in the international psyche.

Yet despite the wealth of material published about the gold rush since that first big strike on Rabbit (later renamed Bonanza) Creek on August 17, 1896, there is still much we do not know about the Klondike. Indeed, there are still historical nuggets waiting to be unearthed that can only add fuel to the hungry fires of our imagination.

One such nugget is Canada's Stikine Route, a forgotten passage to the Klondike that has been largely buried by time and the natural elements. A century ago, the 1,500-kilometre Stikine Route was patriotically known as the all-Canadian route to the goldfields. It wasn't Canada's only trail; several difficult overland routes fanned out from Edmonton, attracting some 1,500 gold seekers. But the Stikine Route was far and away the most popular one, travelled by an estimated five thousand rugged souls between the winter of 1897 and the fall of 1898. Their journey began in northwestern British Columbia with a trip up the Stikine River—either by ice sled in winter or by stern-wheel boat in spring and summer—to the bookend communities of Glenora and Telegraph Creek. The hopefuls then hiked almost due north over the Stikine Plateau on the Teslin Trail to Teslin Lake on the Yukon border, where they began the final leg of their journey, a trip by boat, canoe or raft down Teslin Lake, the Teslin River and finally the Yukon River to Dawson.

The majority of the gold seekers, an estimated 20,000 to 30,000, took either of two principal routes through Alaska at Skagway and Dyea, climbing up and over the rigorous Chilkoot or White passes to the upper reaches of the Yukon River watershed at Bennett and Lindeman lakes, just inside the British Columbia border. Then they built their own boats or rafts from standing shoreline timber and floated downstream to Dawson in a ragtag flotilla launched with the breakup of the ice in the spring of 1898. These are the two routes whose memory is kept alive today in Dawson and Skagway through national historic trails, gambling casinos and can-can dancehalls: tourist gold mines that continue to generate more revenue than did even the first gold diggings.

Canada's Stikine Route enjoys no such recognition. No historical societies are fighting for its preservation. No throngs of cash-ready tourists are lining up to experience its rich history. In effect, the Stikine Route has been wiped from the Canadian map as effectively as chalk from a blackboard. In the summer of 1992, I planned to change all that. Over a six-week period, I took it as my own personal mission to rekindle the spirit of the Stikine Route, to set the record straight, to restore the all-Canadian trail to its rightful place in history. Perhaps it was only fool's gold, or, more accurately, only a fool's idea, but I became possessed by the goal of reliving the spirit of that era and becoming the first person in recent history to retrace this historic route. In the process I would learn something of myself and something of the rigours gold miners faced a century before me.

I was not the first person with such dreams. Almost a decade before my own wilderness odyssey, some eighty members of the First Battalion of the Royal Canadian Regiment retraced parts of the Stikine Route. Their journey had distinctly military roots. They sought to follow in the steps of the members of the Yukon Field Force who took the Stikine Route in 1898 to display a Canadian presence before an army of American miners invading the Yukon. In the summer of 1983, these modern military men were flown by Hercules aircraft to Watson Lake, Yukon, and bussed south to Telegraph Creek, where they began the overland hike to Teslin Lake, armed with modern means of communication but navigating with only map and compass. When they rendezvoused half way with their chartered Beaver floatplane bringing fresh supplies, a handful of soldiers were flown out suffering from a variety of ailments including fever and sore feet. At Teslin Lake, the company was supplied with motorized inflatable boats for the trip down the rivers to Dawson.

Although my trip was, by comparison, an ambitious, bare-bones solo attempt to cover the entirety of the Stikine Route, I rarely travelled alone. The Stikine Route may have been abandoned by history, but it is still home to the sort of rugged individuals who are drawn inexorably to the wildest and remotest stretches of the planet. These individuals—gold miners, fishermen, homesteaders, guide-outfitters, wilderness enthusiasts and descendants of the first aboriginal settlers of this land—kept me company through much of my journey, sharing their campfires and warming my heart with tales of the North: how it attracts them, how it frustrates them and how it is has changed in the century since the last great gold rush. But my journey would also expose me to periods of abject isolation and monumental personal challenge, periods in which I would be tested as surely as those original Klondikers were tested a century before me on this same route. There would be times when the once-famous Stikine Route would fade without trace into the elements and I would yearn for even the crudest of trails or the brief company of a sourdough at my campsite. Yes, mine was a journey into history, but it was also a very personal odyssey, an exploration of those inexplicable urges—as valid today as a century ago—that propel us to places we'd best not go.

1

THE GREAT RIVER

It is 4:45 p.m., already two hours past high tide, and tides are everything to boaters who ply the shallow glacial waters of the Stikine River delta. Only a narrow passage of water threads the river mouth, and with the onset of an ebb tide, the margin for error closes by the minute. That's what Dick Olson will tell you. And he should know. The fifty-seven-year-old Alaskan once spent all night out on a sandbar in his skiff, as immobile as a bloated seal carcass, exposed to the bitter sweeping rains and unable to contact his family before high tide mercifully returned to release him. "I thought I knew the channel," he recalls with a lingering shudder. "But I was ten feet from where I should have been. I stepped out and it was up to the soles of my shoes. It was hours before I could lift off again." Around these parts, falling prey to the sticky tentacles of the Stikine delta is less a source of embarrassment than a rite of passage. "These things happen and there is nothing in the world I could do about it," Dick confirms. "Almost everyone goes through it."

Alaskan expediter Dick Olson and his pooch Lindy stop for a break on their regular run, delivering food and supplies to Great Glacier Salmon Co-op, a fish camp on the Stikine River, just inside the British Columbia border. (Larry Pynn)

Life is full of interesting and unexpected experiences we'd rather not repeat, and getting stuck in the Stikine delta is among them. Perhaps that explains why Dick is pacing so nervously outside my phone booth. A commercial expediter and the father of five girls and four boys, he is anxious to make the fifty-kilometre run safely from his home in the Alaska Panhandle port of Wrangell to Great Glacier Salmon, a fish-processing co-operative just inside Canadian territory at the confluence of the Stikine and Iskut rivers. Although Dick has done the trip twenty-two times this year alone, it never

Wilderness travellers heading up the Stikine River from the Alaskan port of Wrangell earlier this century had to deal with a bare-bones Canada Customs office just downstream of the Iskut River on the Canadian–American border. (B.C. Archives and Records Service)

becomes routine, never a foregone certainty: not the scenery, as grand as any on earth, not the close encounters with moose and bear, and especially not the sprawling delta and its shifting web of sand.

On this overcast late-July afternoon, the cause for delay is Dick's rather unusual manifest. That would be me. I am on the telephone to a Canada Customs inspector in the British Columbia city of Prince Rupert, almost three hundred kilometres to the south, trying to explain why I have chosen to return to Canada via this unusual port of entry. What can I say? That I am a wilderness gladiator, fighting my way up the Stikine River with the tenacity of a spawning salmon? That Dick is my first ticket on a 1,500-kilometre, one-way odyssey across some of the most remote stretches of the Canadian North? That I am going for the gold, following the century-old Stikine Route to the Klondike goldfields, a route that has been neglected by history, ravaged by the forces of nature and all but swallowed up by the passage of time? No, I don't think so. When it comes to customs inspectors, it is best to keep it simple, arouse as little suspicion as possible. Better yet, let Dick do the talking. He is the expediter, isn't he? As a regular traveller across the international border via the Stikine River, bringing provisions to the Great Glacier fishing camp with the predictability of a zookeeper at feeding time, he knows these customs boys as well as he knows his marine charts. A friendly voice from unfamiliar territory, he grabs the telephone receiver and addresses the inspector directly.

I step out of the phone booth and onto the harbour dock, suck up the briny sea air, and muse briefly on this tiny island port. My stay will be far too short. I arrived only thirty minutes ago at the

airport on an Alaska Airlines flight from Anchorage and already
have one foot in a boat headed up the Stikine River. That has pretty
much always been the case for arrivals in Wrangell. Traditionally,
this place has been not so much a destination as a pit stop for
travellers going somewhere else, be it the prospector struggling
toward the Klondike goldfields a century ago or today's pampered
cruise-ship passenger headed for the glacial fjords farther up the
Inside Passage.

Wrangell has changed hands as many times as a two-bit placer
mine, coming under the control of four nations in less than two
centuries: first the Tlingits, a trade-conscious tribe of coastal Indians;
then the Russians, operating as the Russian-American Company in
1834 (Wrangell takes its name from an early governor of the company); next the Hudson's Bay Company, which hoisted the British
flag over Wrangell in 1840 and named it Fort Stikine after signing
a fur-trading lease with the Russians; and finally the Americans,
who put an end to British influence by purchasing Alaska from
the Russians for a measly $7.2 million in 1867 in one of North
America's greatest real-estate bargains.

Wrangell's boom-and-bust economy had a connection to Canadian
gold mining as early as 1861, a full thirty-five years before the big
Klondike strike, when the community served as a commercial hub
and staging area for a short-lived rush on the Stikine River near
Telegraph Creek and again in the Cassiar Mountains in 1873, a
strike that prompted the British Columbia government to construct
a pack trail some one hundred kilometres from Telegraph Creek
to Dease Lake. One of the few persons who stayed around long
enough to get to know the place in those days was the legendary

*Reports of the Alaskan port of Wrangell, at the mouth of the
Stikine River, from a century ago were invariably bad, including
American naturalist John Muir's description of a "lawless draggle
of wooden huts and houses.* (B.C. Archives and Records Service)

John Muir, one of America's early naturalist adventurers. He spent
several months in Wrangell in 1879, exploring the area's forests and
glaciers and rivers and making regular forays up the Stikine River
into Canadian territory. Wrangell wasn't much to look at back then,
just a pathetic, ramshackle settlement, with Tlingit Indians at both
ends of the village, white tradesmen in the middle. "Wrangell village was a rough place," Muir wrote. "The most inhospitable place
at first sight I had ever seen. No mining hamlet in the placer gulches

of California, nor any backwoods village I ever saw, approached it in picturesque, devil-may-care abandon. It was a lawless draggle of wooden huts and houses, built in crooked lines, wrangling around the boggy shore of the island for a mile or so in the general form of the letter S, without the slightest subordination to the points of the compass or to building laws of any kind. There was nothing like a tavern or lodging house in the village, nor could I find any place in the stumpy, rocky, boggy ground about it that looked dry enough to camp on...."

That this rambunctious runt of a town, scarcely even a community and located in American waters at that, should serve as the jumping-off point for the all-Canadian Stikine route to Dawson City is one of the great ironies of the Klondike gold rush. But history is rife with irony. Should the Klondike be different? Under terms of the British-Russian Convention of 1825, British subjects in the Canadian provinces had the right to free navigation up the Stikine River. In reality, however, the deep-draught, oceangoing steamboats had to transship cargo and passengers to the flat-bottomed stern-wheelers at the mouth of the Stikine River. That put Wrangell in a position of strategic commercial importance—a natural port and a last-chance stop for mining provisions. As such, it was a much busier town during the Klondike gold rush than when Muir knew it, but no better organized. A meal cost thirty-five cents, hotel accommodation one to two dollars to a day. The harbour bustled with activity. Tlingit Indians shot coastal Sitka black-tailed deer and sold them as venison to miners for $3.50 to $5.00 apiece. And the town was ruled by crooks and con men who worked the miners' pockets until they held little more than lint. Indeed, the port was about as

In a twist of irony, the Alaskan port of Wrangell served as the jumping-off point for the Canadian route to the Klondike. Here, at the mouth of the Stikine River, ship passengers from Vancouver and Victoria switched to flat-bottomed stern-wheelers for the trip to Telegraph Creek. (B.C. Archives and Records Service)

savoury as day-old fish guts or freshly stained creosote, symbolic perhaps of the cultural chasm that existed between brash America and reserved Canada during the frontier era. As a seventeen-year-old greenhorn Brit, Guy Lawrence followed the Stikine route in 1898 before launching into a lengthy career on the Yukon telegraph line. "Before we landed, notices had been posted in various parts of the ship, warning us that Wrangell was a very tough port, indeed," he wrote. "Above all, we were told not to associate with strangers." Of course, for a teenager, danger is just another word for adventure. "They were to me exciting days with guns popping all the time, the constant barking and howling of dogs, mostly everybody in good spirits."

Among the more dramatic visitors to Wrangell in 1898 were 203 members of the Yukon Field Force, an ad hoc unit of the Canadian Militia travelling with two Maxim machine guns and two old seven-pounder field guns. The Dominion Government had sent the soldiers north to enforce Canadian law and protect Canadian sovereignty in the face of tens of thousands of American gold seekers roaming the territory. Given the patriotic nature of their assignment, the soldiers naturally travelled the Stikine route rather than the American-held Chilkoot and White passes to reach their assigned postings at Fort Selkirk and Dawson on the Yukon River. Theirs would be a short-lived assignment; half the soldiers were withdrawn a year later as the Boer War raged in South Africa, and the others were recalled in 1900. As the Klondike gold rush quickly sputtered out, practicalities prevailed over patriotism and the soldiers took the more immediate routes home through U.S. territory.

Faith Fenton, a correspondent for the Toronto *Globe* on a sort of journalistic ride-along with the soldiers, found Wrangell to be a quirky place that lived for the moment. "The chief hotel—a really good establishment for the place—is two months old; the majority of shops are four weeks old; while the residences, tents and shacks can be reckoned by weeks. There are no streets—each building, shack or tent, has squatted at will and everybody strolls through everybody else's backyard."

A century later, Wrangell is a community of 3,000, a relative model of friendliness and civility. When Dick's teenaged daughter, Tami, picked me up at the airport and dropped me off at the dock to await her father, I asked what to do with my backpack and supplies while I shopped. "This town is very small," she replied quietly. "You can leave your stuff on the dock. No one will take it." And no one did.

Modern Wrangell is dominated by the forest industry and fishing, but some businesses are still servicing Canadian mining activity in the Golden Triangle, a region of gold-rich properties up the Iskut River. Tourism plays an increasing role in the economy; the Alaska ferry system makes a regular stop, as do the cruise ships in summer, and an ecotourism industry is developing the town as a jumping-off point for recreational fishing and wilderness hiking. I am happy to report, however, that Wrangell still has its quirks. The town's sawmill closes for maintenance during both the spring salmon derby and the fall moose hunt rather than try to operate with an absentee workforce. The community is closer by air to Seattle, Washington, than to Anchorage, Alaska's largest city to the north. And the annual Tent City Festival, a three-day celebration of the town's role during the Klondike gold rush, is held in February to provide relief from the winter blahs.

I would like to have more time to spend in Wrangell. I would like to walk among the great Tlingit totems on Front Street; quaff a beer at the Brig Bar, where former football star Rosie Grier tossed a man through a window during the filming of the movie *Timber Tramps*; or hop a Porky's Cab to Fool's Inlet, just for the hell of it. But Dick is off the phone now and bounding down the dock. The Stikine awaits. Firing up the seventy-horsepower outboard motor on his six-metre-long aluminum skiff, Dick makes one final check for his other travelling companion: Lindy, a cocker spaniel-rottweiler cross, and presumably undeclared cargo. "She's not good for much," he concedes. "Except for chasing bears. She can spot them a mile away."

Like so many Northerners, Dick makes a living from various jobs. Trained in explosive engineering ("It's all mathematics"), he worked twenty years in banking, most recently as president of the Bank of Petersburg in a small Alaskan port community about forty-five kilometres to the north, until, exhibiting typical Northern independence, he decided to get out rather than "kiss ass." Besides his expediting company, he runs a motel, bar and fish-guiding business, and there are plans for a river-rafting operation on the Stikine. Earlier this morning, he woke up at 3 a.m. to lead tourists on a dawn run to Anan Creek, a popular spot for watching black bears and grizzlies gorge on spawning pink salmon.

As we pull away from the Wrangell dock and the strip of low-rise waterfront buildings, the nature of my expedition begins to take hold. I am flooded with memories of a lifetime of close calls, like the time, at age sixteen, when I scooped up three friends in my fibreglass runabout and sped off without a compass or chart or brains into the thick Strait of Georgia fog off Vancouver and remained lost there for hours before nature took pity on us and released us back to our worried parents; at twenty-nine, cross-country skiing in Kootenay National Park in the Rocky Mountains when a cornice of snow broke off high overhead, thundered down the rock bluff, and nearly buried me alive; at thirty-four, after viewing a Bill Mason how-to-canoe-white-water videotape, paddling down the Spatsizi and upper Stikine rivers—and taking my nineteen-year-old nephew, Brian, with me. And one year ago, at thirty-six, hiking 275 kilometres through the Mackenzie Mountains of the Northwest Territories and almost drowning while crossing the Twitya River, exhausted, in a snowstorm.

These memories cannot help but shape my feelings as I embark on my most ambitious adventure of all. Experience has made me a wiser outdoorsman. But it has also taught me that adventure is a narcotic and that anyone who seriously seeks it is vulnerable to the addiction. Close calls can embolden a person to attempt greater heights, more dangerous challenges. Ultimately, it is wasting your breath to tell people to know their limits when only through failure can they realize them. But I also speculate: how many gold miners leaving Wrangell a century ago shared similar doubts about their own abilities and wondered if the route ahead was paved with gold—or strewn with disappointment and hardship?

"Presumably there's twenty feet below us now," Dick remarks with a quick look over the side of the boat. "The glacial water is so murky, you can't see anything. If we tried to go straight we wouldn't make it. I guarantee it." The old riverboat captains used to talk of "walking" their stern-wheelers over the shallows of the delta, an equally nerve-wracking process for passengers who were keen on reaching the goldfields and not wanting to become stranded on a sandbar. "I'd love to have been around a hundred years ago," comments Dick, not fazed by the physical hardships the Klondikers had to endure. "I've still got gold fever. I've panned for gold until my fingers bled." He fishtails his way through the south arm of the Stikine delta along an informal route marked by islands and detergent bottles, confident—sort of—that we are on course. We pass a commercial dredge on a barge, a reflection of just how much silt flows down the Stikine, then spot a collection of duck-hunting shacks on the shoreline of Sergief Island, named after a member of the Russian navy who drowned during an expedition up the Stikine River in 1863. "See that one?" Dick says, pointing to a shack higher up the beach than the rest. "They floated it in on a twenty-two-foot tide and couldn't get it off. I don't know how they'll do it."

Just up ahead lies Cottonwood Island, an unpopulated, dagger-like stretch of land that a century ago swarmed with would-be gold miners and their pack animals and provisions, all destined for the Klondike diggings. Stern-wheelers operated a shuttle service for miners between Wrangell and Cottonwood Island, a distance of about fifteen kilometres, charging $5 a ton for freight and $2.50 a passenger, compared with $25 for the five-day trip from Vancouver. Tents covered the island like spruce trees, dogs howled into the night and tempers frayed as an international cast jockeyed for position. "Everything appeared to be in a muddle," Klondiker Stratford Tollemache wrote of Cottonwood Island. "Altercations and brawls were occasionally intermingled with free fights, and these, mixed with the howling of the dogs, created a perfect pandemonium."

For those miners who spent winter on the Stikine route to Klondike goldfields, home was a simple hand-hewn log cabin with a sod roof. Dogs were used for transport, packing, and, no doubt, companionship during the dark winter months. (B.C. Archives and Records Service)

Miners arrived at the Stikine River with enough supplies to last months. Camp outfitters in Victoria and Vancouver competed fiercely for sales of clothing, tents, stoves, picks, axes, livestock feed, canvas boats, shovels, cutlery. Among the more unusual food items were soup tablets, evaporated potatoes, Russell's Empress Cream —"none other will stand the test of the Alaska climate"—and LaMont's Improved Crystallized Egg—"most nourishing food for Alaska." A miner also needed a rifle along the route to hunt for moose, caribou, waterfowl and grouse. "A Winchester rifle, the watchdog for the Klondike," read one advertisement. "It bites when it barks. It will protect your claim and supply you with food." Perhaps the strangest product, touted as a Klondike staple, was Dr. Sanden's Electric Belt. The sales pitch went like this: "This is an electric life giver. It saturates the nerves and muscles with animal magnetism, which is the life force that builds up weak constitutions. It is a wonderful life giver and no man who is doubtful of his physical vigor should go without it."

Prospectors who arrived in Wrangell during the winter hauled their supplies up the river ice on sleds, a tedious process accomplished bit by bit through repeated trips. But that winter of 1897-98 proved to be unusually mild, forcing miners to break camp well before daylight when the cooler temperatures created a good crust for pulling the sleds. As winter yielded to spring, the trail became a sticky slush and sledding a gut-wrenching chore, with the added risk of falling through the ice. Some miners found it too much to bear and returned, demoralized, to Wrangell, abandoning some of their provisions on the trail and selling the rest for whatever the precarious market would allow.

Under such extreme physical conditions, the pack animals suffered abominable cruelty. Underfed and overworked, they were pushed and beaten to the point of collapse. Horses sank to their haunches in the wet snow or fell through the ice, only to be tied by the tail and hauled out by other horses so that the horrendous ordeal could begin anew. Man's best friend the dog fared no better. One miner started out with twelve dogs and ended with two; as each dropped dead, it was boiled and fed to the survivors.

Along the river, miners huddled in their tents next to their portable stoves, gnawing on dried meat, biscuits and beans and hoping the whole place would not go up in flames, as some occasionally did, leaving them buck naked to the world. John Deeks was among a party of six heading north from Cottonwood Island that winter, arriving in Telegraph Creek six weeks later, just before the breakup of ice. "Observations along the way are glaciers here and there, occasionally a dead horse or dog, dangerous ice and narrow escapes," he recorded in his diary. "Camps or caches always in sight. Small talk is condition of the roads and distances and mostly profanity. Horses, dogs often worked to death. Personally I have become naturalized, my hands sore swollen and cracked, my feet blistered and sore, my ears nipped with frost and peeling, my face very much burnt and tanned by the sun. I changed my undershirt and found lice galore. I stripped everything and boiled all my underclothes and had a sponge bath." For Deeks, at least, the ordeal paid off. He worked a profitable placer claim at Atlin for five years, sold it for $75,000 and set himself up in the moneymaking sand-and-gravel business at Porteau, on Howe Sound north of Vancouver.

An artist's account of the monumental hardships miners faced hauling their supplies up the Stikine River on the Canadian route to the Klondike in the winter of 1897–98. (B.C. Archives and Records Service)

His name is today preserved on a plaque at Porteau, a provincial park campsite, and in Deeks Lake and Deeks Creek, flowing into Howe Sound on the Squamish Highway.

Other miners at Cottonwood Island waited for spring breakup to make their way upriver, either as fare-paying passengers aboard the first steam paddle wheelers or aboard their own small craft, some of these purchased and some handhewed from the shoreline timber. Getting upriver demanded poling, lining with ropes from shore and paddling through the fast-flowing streams and over the confounded gravel bars. It was the poor man's way to the goldfields for sure, and many a pitiful soul drowned or froze to death or died of scurvy before the Klondike had a chance to dash his hopes forever.

As Dick and I proceed up the Stikine past Cottonwood Island in relative luxury, we are leaving one of the richest river deltas in North America, a home to millions of life-forms: bald eagles congregating for the annual spawning runs of greasy oolichans; juvenile salmon milling about in the intertidal foreshore, making the transition from fresh water to salty ocean; and shorebirds on the Pacific flyway, fuelling up for their spring flight to breeding grounds farther north in Alaska or for their return trip each fall to wintering grounds as distant as South America. No wonder the early Tlingits labelled it the Great River.

Then, with the suddenness of an orgasm, Dick lights up a cigarette and announces that we are free of the delta's grip. "We're clear now. Want to go to the hot springs?" Hot springs? Did the Klondikers have time for such luxuries? Slogging upstream on an ice sled could take a month or more in the bitter cold. Even the stern-wheelers could take a week or more to reach Glenora, stopping for wood supplies and winching their way through the toughest stretches of water. Time was money. Those who delayed in their quest would almost certainly lose out on the best gold diggings. Do I want to bother with such a frivolous sideshow? Do I want to divert my single-minded attention from the Stikine route? Bloody right I do.

Chief Shakes (the name taken by a succession of Tlingit leaders) hot springs flows from the north side of the river, still within American territory and hiding away down a narrow slough. Dick gently idles his way through the shallow waters, checking for depth

Toronto newspaper correspondent Faith Fenton (third from the left) poses beside Rev. John Pringle outside a general store in Glenora, the central encampment for miners on the Stikine River headed north on the Teslin Trail in 1898. (B.C. Archives and Records Service)

and direction. He hits bottom momentarily, propeller vomiting out sand and mud, before we continue, eventually pulling ashore under a canopy of cottonwoods, leaves glistening like a silver chime in the late evening sun.

A short walk takes us to a mosquito-infested marsh crisscrossed with moose tracks. The thick coastal underbrush in southeast Alaska makes hunters employ a unique stalking technique: they sit quietly in a tree by a marsh and wait to pop the first moose that comes along. No, it's not hunting in the true sense. But what is? Much hunting these days is done by pickup truck, a couple of buddies roaming logging roads and dirt tracks until an animal makes the mistake of crossing the road. Dick confirms the incongruity of Alaska's version. "I was sitting in a tree one day when another hunter walked up and said, 'Hey, that's my tree! Everyone knows that's my tree!'" When Dick refused to budge, the hunter went off a short way, then fired several shots to scare off any potential moose. "I never went back there again," says Dick, shaking his head.

Just ahead, mist rises from the marsh like steam off a pig's back. A wisp of low cloud teases its way across an alpine slope. Shakes Glacier, above and beyond, glistens like an aboriginal icon. And the murmurs of a young couple percolate from an outdoor hot tub. As we join them in the warm, soothing mineral springs, Dick cannot help but reflect, "We're a bunch of wimps. The miners were the real tough ones." It is unlikely that gold miners who did visit the hot springs had the luxury of staying long. The lure of the river, the promise of gold, the pending breakup of the river ice all drove them on. As it does ourselves. It is already 8 p.m., and after a short dip we continue our trip, anxious to reach Great Glacier Salmon camp before dark.

Returning to Dick's boat, we steer out of the slough and proceed upriver past a landscape little changed since the gold rush, protected as it is in Alaska from mining and clear-cut logging by the Stikine-LeConte Wilderness. With each passing glacial creek, the Stikine flexes its muscles, spitting out two-metre-wide whirlpools. Watching from the sidelines, the Coast Mountains grow tall from the riverbank, their flanks covered by lush forests watered by an abundant rainfall averaging 200 centimetres a year. The land is a rich, temperate landscape teeming with moose and bear, terrestrial expatriates that have spilled over from Canadian territory.

The mountain tops have a rough, crumpled look, like molten lead after cooling. Glaciers drip down the slopes like dollops of thick white icing. And the river is a web of channels. This is a vastly different river from the Upper Stikine I canoed three years ago with my nephew. As the upper river passes along the northern edge of Spatsizi Plateau Wilderness Park, it is a solid powerful body of water, alternating between swollen pools and hair-raising stretches of pure white water. It is a roller-coaster ride in which the safety of the uphill climb is inevitably followed by the exhilarating danger of the downhill run. Here, on the lower stretches of the Stikine, it is different but no less dangerous. "It's the fastest-flowing navigable river in North America," Dick assures me. "I never get tired of it."

An occasional sweeper tree hangs horizontally from the clay banks, waiting to decapitate the first careless boater. And sticks are forever protruding from the silty-grey water like twitching, half-dead hands, reaching out to ensnare boaters. Sand dunes loom on our right, an image of the delta's past life, where strong headwinds of sixty to seventy knots can whip up, blinding boaters and sometimes forcing them to take shelter. Then we pass an aluminum skiff, abandoned and buried arrow-like in the sand bank. "It came down from the Canadian side," Dick offers tersely. "You wonder what happened to the people." Occasionally, someone wanders out of the wilderness, too, like a ghost from the last gold rush. "I met a Swiss fellow once, walking down the mountain. He hadn't eaten in days. Was he glad to see me."

Minutes later, Dick points out a distinct logging slash through the forest running up and over the next mountain: the official border between Alaska and British Columbia. Yes, you could call it a monument to bureaucracy and a waste of good trees. But, in a world of increasing tribal warfare, where borders are still defended with guns and bunkers and razor wire, this simple green vein through the forest reveals far more about our nations than the Parliamentary Channel or Hansard. "The border is right there," Dick confirms. "Just three miles to camp."

2

THE SALMON RUSH

Great Glacier Salmon Co-op has a Cannery Row look to it. Even the shortest walk is an adventure, whether up the rickety steps, around the fuel drums, past the moose antlers, or through the bushes. There is nothing flat or straight or stable in the whole place. The boardwalk outside my room resembles a suspension bridge. When someone swaggers down it, the bed shakes and the mosquito netting sways overhead, as though I were sleeping on a geological fault. The place exudes an offbeat connection to its environment, too, its very existence owed to the earth and the sky and the water. Hacked out of the humid, temperate rain forest, the fish camp clings tenaciously to a 150-metre strip of riverbank, fortified by giant stands of spruce and hemlock. It even owes its power to the rain gods. Almost every activity in camp is governed by the volume of water flowing through a handmade, forty-seven-kilowatt power dam located a tough, 530-metre slog up the mountainside. The interconnectedness of the place is highlighted by a funny sign in the camp mess hall: "Don't use the toaster unless it rains."

23

With the Coast Mountains as a backdrop, members of Great Glacier Salmon Co-op driftnet fish on the lower Stikine River, just inside the British Columbia border with Alaska. (Larry Pynn)

The fish-processing plant looms over the Stikine River on wooden stilts—a big praying mantis, unflinching, unbreathing, yet somehow alive and bristling with intent. On the shoreline beneath it, fishermen motor up in aluminum drift boats and attach steel cables to fish-laden totes. Once hoisted to a platform above, the totes are transferred to the processing plant, where the heads of the salmon are guillotined, the bodies disembowelled and the guts flushed into the river and the bellies of well-fed harbour seals. Bright red eggs from the females are transferred to white buckets for shipment to Seattle, en route to the pricier markets of Europe as caviar. The rest of the fish, glazed in a solution of water, sugar and salt, is frozen within twelve hours of being caught, then stacked like cordwood in a cold-storage room.

"We're the only fishing company that delivers half of its catch to the plant alive," boasts Bob Gould, the corporate and spiritual leader of Great Glacier. "It's been a million-dollar investment. Triple that, with sweat equity." Bob's tousled grey locks, piercing, glacier-blue eyes, stubble of beard, mackinaw and rain gear only hint at his personality. At forty-seven, he is a philosopher, cynic and river rogue, perfect attributes for someone in such an unorthodox place. He is also an ex-military intelligence officer; but he won't talk about that, and you wouldn't expect him to do otherwise. "If you write that, I'll send the vigilantes after you," he jokes.

Leading me to his "condo"—his cluttered, but funky, sleepy quarters—he hands me a Corona beer and talks about the new currency on the Stikine River, the Pacific salmon. "Nobody makes money in a gold rush," he asserts, quick to draw a connection between his personal odyssey and my own. "Maybe four out of forty thousand." He is right, to a degree. A century ago in the Klondike, only the lucky few who got in early and staked the best streams walked away rich. Thousands of others who wagered the shirts off their backs to get to Dawson City found the gold already claimed and their dreams dashed. Today it is not much different. Too often it is the unscrupulous Vancouver Stock Exchange promoter who walks away the winner and the small investor who pays the price. But it is also true that all the false hopes and false alarms have done nothing to tarnish people's lust for gold. And nowhere is that truer than here, in British Columbia's Golden Triangle. Over the past half-dozen years, a gold-rush mentality has dominated the region, doing for prime, gold-bearing streams such as Eskay Creek what the Klondike did a century ago for Bonanza and Eldorado. For now, at least, gold, not salmon, is still the big player in the watershed of the Stikine River.

That doesn't stop Bob from dreaming. To him, salmon is the soul of the river. That is what drew him here to the edge of civilization a dozen years ago. That is what keeps him here. It is also the first resource of the Stikine River, the one that enticed the Tlingit Indians to settle in this wildlife-rich corner of the continent. The delta of the Stikine provided a bountiful supply of food for those early aboriginal inhabitants, something that didn't go unnoticed by the first white visitors to the region. Clive Phillips-Wolley, an adventurous big-game hunter who visited the Stikine River in 1895, just a year before the big Klondike strike, wrote of two Tlingit Indians killing fifty deer, two wolves and a bear in a two-week hunting trip on the islands around Wrangell. Migrating waterfowl were seasonally bountiful in the Stikine delta and halibut grew to immense proportions. But it was the annual summer return of Pacific salmon that chiefly sustained the Tlingit people. They made seasonal treks up the Stikine in their giant cedar dugout canoes to

Bob and Celine Gould are the principals of Great Glacier Salmon Co-op, a fishing and processing plant built in the early 1980s to compete with Alaskans for Canadian-spawned fish. (Larry Pynn)

drier portions of the river, on the lee side of the Coast Mountains, to gaff salmon from rocks jutting out from the river and to cure the fish in the heat of campfire smoke and the summer sun.

The Stikine's rich waters were not entirely overlooked by the Klondikers, either. They bartered with the Tlingits and the Tahltans, who lived farther upriver, for salmon or caught their own as the opportunity arose. Describing Wrangell as a shanty town of "hibernating miners and fish-eating Indians," Phillips-Wolley noted that a white man's cannery stood at the mouth of the Stikine and there were Indian drying racks on the riverbanks. "The toll these take seems to make no difference," he wrote. "Year after year the little streams are full of ill-formed, hook-nosed monsters, rotting as they swim, crimson with corruption, or colourless as they drift downstream, tails upward, dead and decomposing."

Unlike gold, Bob Gould has concluded, salmon can theoretically be extracted from these unblemished waters year after year, a precious resource that is never exhausted. He came to that conclusion a decade ago after participating in a federal-provincial project surveying fish-bearing streams in the lower Stikine area, checking for depth, velocity, turbidity, temperature. "We walked every stream, as far as the salmon could go," he says with lingering satisfaction. "We also looked for grizzlies, bald eagles, trout." The experience convinced him that to preserve the salmon is to preserve the future of the Great River. "A mile of good spawning gravel," he says confidently, "is worth more than any mine in the history of Canada."

Great Glacier's roots go back to 1979. B.C. Packers, the Vancouver-based fish-processing giant, received a federal subsidy to kick-start the fishery and venture into the remote Stikine wilderness to deliver Great Glacier's salmon catch to market. At the same time, the fisheries department sought out parties interested in starting a commercial fishery on the lower Stikine River. Bob and a handful of friends were among those who took up the offer, arriving with little more than their pup tents and Coleman stoves to stake their claim on the lip of the Canadian wilderness. Bob had a solid knowledge of the Stikine River, having written an Honours paper in International Studies in 1972 at Simon Fraser University on the subject of American encroachment on Canadian sovereignty on the northern transboundary rivers. Oh yes, he had one more reason for being here. "We chose the Stikine because there is no basis for native land claims all the way up to Telegraph Creek," he says. "The Tlingits decided they would be Alaskans." Over the ensuing years, the federal government offered financial assistance for freighting subsidies, the hiring of a native worker and camp construction. The fishermen shipped in materials to build bunks, the mess hall, work shop, processing plant, eventually even an office with a computer. Bob is especially proud of the hydro dam. "We'd haul eighty pounds of cement on our backpacks. Rebar, everything. That's why it took three years." In those early days, greedy Alaskan gill-net fishermen downstream were the enemy, thumbing their noses at the principle that salmon belong to their country of origin—an argument the Americans had themselves used against Japanese fishermen harvesting United States-spawned salmon in the North Pacific. Ignoring every concept of fairness, the Alaskans wanted it all. And they might have succeeded except for a Canadian presence on the river. During the Klondike gold rush, the Yukon Field Force protected Canadian sovereignty against an invasion of American prospectors. Almost a century later, it was up to Bob—described by one federal fisheries officer as a "pirate and a businessman to the nth degree"—and his ragtag armada to represent Canada's interests. "An Alaskan fisherman said, 'When it comes down to it, how many nuclear subs do you have?'" Bob recalls with relish, "so I replied: 'How is England doing in Northern Ireland?'"

When Canada decided to start commercial fishing on the Stikine River, regardless of what the Americans thought, it got their attention. After all, with two countries going their own way on one river, it was only a matter of time before the salmon stocks would decline and both parties would end up losers. The resolution to the stalemate came in 1985 with the signing of the Pacific Salmon Treaty between Canada and the United States and an annex for the transboundary rivers. The agreement broke down two years later when the annex expired; but negotiations continued, and both parties heralded a new five-year fishing agreement in 1988. The deal was far from perfect. For example, although 85 percent of the Stikine traverses Canadian soil and 100 percent of the sockeye spawn in Canadian waters, Canadian fishermen would take just 27 percent of the 1992 estimated harvest of 106,000 sockeye. But at least the deal helps to preserve and enhance salmon stocks and gives Canada some reason to hope future talks can reach agreement on a straight fifty-fifty spilt on sockeye, the dominant commercial catch on the river.

For Great Glacier, signing of the treaty just refocused the struggle. One year later, in 1986, the federal government, deciding to even the odds, granted a subsidy to the Tahltan Indians from Telegraph Creek to start their own fish camp on the lower Stikine. Alaskan fishermen were no longer the enemy; Canadians were competing against each other for a relatively small share of the total run. To inflame the situation further, Stephan Jacob, a non-native and co-founder of Great Glacier, accepted a job with the Tahltan camp. Those were ugly days. Opposing factions struggled for the

His parents run Great Glacier Salmon Co-op, but eleven-year-old Kevin Gould would rather try his own luck fishing at dusk on the lower Stikine River in remote northwestern British Columbia. (Larry Pynn)

best fishing spots. Fishermen carried guns. Fights broke out. Anger and frustration boiled up all over the river. Great Glacier members even burned their Canadian flag and pissed on the ashes. "We used to be patriotic," Bob reflects bitterly. "We got sold down the tube."

During the summer of my visit to Great Glacier, peace reigns on the Stikine. None of the Tahltan fishermen have even bothered to come downriver to exercise their fishing rights. And part of their fishing camp is submerged in a lagoon on the river. "It's a waste of money," says Bob, motoring me past for a closer look, "but more importantly a waste of people." To which his wife, Celine, adds, "Those fellows used to be our best workers. It's a shame." As for Jacob, jumping ship proved to be a poor career choice. He lost his job with the Tahltans, and Great Glacier took him to court, winning a stinging out-of-court settlement. Jacob proved to be Bob's most satisfying catch—a trophy fish, stuffed and mounted, after years of costly legal fighting. According to the terms of the settlement, every year Jacob must fish one day only. To do that, he has to travel all the way from Salt Spring Island, near Victoria. And he must sell his catch to Great Glacier. Jacob wasn't beaten; he was humiliated. Reflecting later on events, he would concede he'd made a mistake working for the Tahltans. "It's sad, what happened," he said, blaming poor management and discipline for the Tahltans' failure. "I learned that you can't fight someone else's battles. I know that Great Glacier saw me as a traitor, but I thought I was doing something good. I should never have got involved."

Besides Bob and Celine, a charming but passionately determined French Canadian who pretty much runs the camp's finances, Great Glacier consists of their daughter, Jenny, and her husband, Robin

Boucher; plant foreman Billy Larsen, a soft-spoken, cigarette-smoking Tahltan with a gunslinger's black moustache; Doug Blanchard of Francois Lake in British Columbia's Interior, identifiable anywhere on the river by his corncob pipe; and independents Bill and Ruth Sampson, a couple who homestead upriver near Glenora. As for the plant workers, they are as heterogeneous as Canada, a mix of English, French and natives hailing from Montreal, Alberta, Toronto and Saskatchewan, all drawn to the wilderness for ten dollars an hour plus room, board and travel.

The salmon camp derives its name from Great Glacier, a monstrous sky-blue slab of ice flowing like a massive, rough-edged tongue not far upstream on the Stikine. Some 400 years ago, Great Glacier stood at the river's edge but today is a 1.5-kilometre walk away over the glacier's moraine and through a forest dripping with emerald green moss. Arriving with a small party from the fish camp one afternoon, I spot half a dozen Canada geese bobbing among the chunks of broken ice in a lake below the toe of the glacier. Hidden behind a rock is the camp's small, rickety canoe, plastered with duct tape. Billy Larsen is reminded of the time he left the canoe for a short hike and returned to find it a metre and a half farther up the bank, forced there by water displacement when ice calved off the glacier. "If we'd been in it, we could have been finished," he reflects quietly.

John Muir, exploring the area in 1879 on one of his excursions from Wrangell, was similarly surprised by the glacier's potential for violence. "...I was startled by a thundering roar across the lake. Running to the top of the moraine, I discovered that the tremendous noise was only the outcry of a newborn berg about fifty or sixty feet in diameter, rocking and wallowing in the waves it had raised as if enjoying its freedom after its long grinding work as part of the glacier." Other dangers await those who look too closely at the glacier's beauty. A party of Russians who went missing while exploring Great Glacier prior to the sale of Alaska to the United States were believed swallowed up by one of the glacier's deep, ravenous crevasses.

According to native legend, the Stikine River once flowed through a solid vaulted tunnel formed by Great Glacier on one side and Choquette Glacier on the other. Passage beneath was preferable to an arduous hike across the glacier but was fraught with danger. As one story goes, "When the party reached the impasse...two very old women of high caste, together with two equally old men, presented themselves to follow the flow of the waters under the ice bridge. They would attempt the passage and if successful all could follow." In his journals, Muir offers the story with a decidedly different twist: One Indian, anxious to get rid of his wife, sent her through the tunnel in a canoe, only to have her pop out again on the other side.

Although icebergs are occasionally spotted bobbing down the Stikine River, they are by no means the main hazard. That dubious honour falls to the ever-changing gravel bars, mined with driftwood and a constant challenge to the river's fishermen, who employ a drift-net technique in which hundred-metre-long gill nets are set upstream, then allowed to drift back in an arc that catches the salmon migrating upriver. To see for myself, I jump into an eight-metre "bow picker" drift boat with the Goulds and their dog, Spruce, a wiry Jack Russell terrier. Unlike the tree, this Spruce is neither tall nor majestic nor aromatic nor the least bit pleasant to be around. He is a cranky, opossum-sized mutt, about as inviting as devil's club and a match for any bear unfortunate enough to wander into camp. As we set forth from the dock, I cannot help thinking this boat is too small for the two of us.

"You set the net between the snags under the water," Bob explains. "It's a hard-earned art. We go through $25,000 in nets annually." Only a few seconds from camp, we spot a twenty-metre-long log with a huge root system and decide to send it packing downriver before it causes problems. As Bob noses the bow up, Celine crawls forward on her stomach so she can attach a line. "We'd be better off in the logging business than fishing," she says, looking back over her shoulder. "This is 60 percent of fishing the Stikine River. The rest is easy." During periods of low water in the fall, removing snags is even more difficult. Some only get the message with a stick of dynamite.

Celine examines the snag so closely she might as well be sticking her head into the belly of a man-eating shark. This one sports its share of partially digested victims. "It's got net all over it, you bitch. I don't know why, but whenever we hit a snag, I always think of it as a female. A bitch." As Bob works the motor and wheel, the snag writhes violently, almost painfully, in the churning water. The fight is on. He stabs the bow of the skiff headlong into the log, hoping to dislodge it. "She's gonna roll," he says. "Look at it." Sure enough, the rope pulls off. Bob takes another bang at it and the snag almost rears up and into the boat. With a knife held firmly in her right hand, Celine asserts, "My God, that's the biggest monster I've seen. I don't want it to tear my face off." Carefully she ties a second rope, and Bob gives it one more tug before the snag finally, grudgingly, yields to the river.

Enough of this catch-and-release stuff. It is time for some real fishing. The couple unravel the gill net. While they wait, they reminisce about the supposed romance of fishing. "Once, the timing chain broke," she reflects. "We drifted way past the border. We thought the Americans would arrest us for illegal fishing." But that is nothing. Jenny and Robin Boucher once sank a boat downstream and almost drowned in the process, an incident Jenny still cannot talk about.

As choreographed as a Hollywood horror show, the impossible happens. The snag! It's back, surfacing again in one last horrific gasp beside our boat. "Oh my God, the monster again!" Celine exclaims. "It's still there, waiting to eat us up." Bob quickly pulls the net back across the river, out of the snag's grasp, and watches the log drift downstream. "Ha, ha, goodbye." So lifelike are these river monsters, bobbing back and forth to the surface, that one steamboat passenger heading upriver in 1898 fired two shots from his rifle at one before, in embarrassment, he realized his mistake.

The Tahltan Indians might be fish out of water in this summer's commercial fishery, but historically they had it right: simple fish traps positioned to catch the salmon en route to their spawning beds. Muir described one such encounter, farther upstream above Telegraph Creek, that shows the folly of the white man's competitive and costly fishing methods. "I found a band of Tahltan or Stick Indians catching their winter supply of salmon in willow traps, set where the fish are struggling in swift rapids on their way to the spawning grounds. A large supply had already been secured, and of course the Indians were well fed and merry. They were camping in large booths made of poles set on end in the ground, with many binding cross-pieces on which tons of salmon were being dried. The heads were strung on separate poles and the roe packed in willow baskets, all being well smoked from fires in the middle of the floor. The largest of the booths near the bank of the river was about forty feet square. Beds made of spruce and pine bows were spread all around the walls, on which some of the Indians lay asleep; some were braiding ropes, others sitting and lounging, gossiping and courting, while a little boy was swinging in a hammock. All seemed to be light-hearted and jolly, with work enough and wit enough to maintain health and comfort."

Minutes later we are greeted by Gerald Quash, a Telegraph Creek native employed as a federal fisheries guardian. He is a stickler and tells me to get a permit authorizing my presence aboard a commercial fish boat. During the two years I served as commercial fishing reporter for the Vancouver *Sun* I was never asked for such a document. To encounter such by-the-book thinking in these remote surroundings contradicts my understanding of the North. Although fish-camp members don't directly say so, they have little respect for Gerald, whose appointment they view as linked to federal job-initiative policies for natives rather than knowledge of the fishery. Perhaps that is as good a reason as any for him to play it by the book. I make an appointment to spend an afternoon accompanying Quash on his enforcement rounds on the river, but he does not show up. Alone against a fishing fleet that shows him only grudging respect, Gerald spends most of his off-hours at his government cabin just downstream of Great Glacier, near the old Boundary House customs post. The only peep from him is the crack of gunfire one evening, presumably a last-chance warning for black bears to keep their distance.

Indeed, bear sightings are a regular occurrence around the fish camp. One morning, I am in my room when Bob excitedly beckons me to the riverbank. I run so fast over the bumpy ground for a look that I twist my ankle, raising the worry that such an injury could hamper the hiking portion of my odyssey in the coming days. When I finally hobble to the shoreline, I see a grizzly sow with three second-year cubs across the river on a sandbank. It is warm and sunny, and the cubs chase gulls while the mother saunters casually upriver. The water level has dropped in the past few days, and the four feed on lush new grasses. Bear triplets are a good sign, indicative of just how productive this wilderness can be. Too productive, sometimes. Bears spotted on the camp side of the river are not the least bit endearing and risk being "shipped to Wrangell," a euphemism for being shot and summarily dumped into the river.

When a black bear is spotted one evening in the bushes directly behind the plant, I plead for clemency. For one thing, the bear is eating berries and seemingly uninterested in the salmon. For another, I have an alternative to gunfire—a can of pepper spray—and I am only too happy to try it. With some reservations, Bob agrees to the idea and accompanies me into the forest. Stopping behind a tree trunk twenty metres from the bear, he too has a request. For himself. He cannot resist testing a shot of the stuff first. Reaching for the spray, he removes the orange safety tag and slowly but firmly squeezes the trigger in the direction of his palm. Thwack! A powerful burst of orange bounces off his palm and back into his eyes.

Fighting back tears, Bob returns the spray to me, a little less scep-
tical of the substance than he was a few seconds before.

Now I walk carefully toward the bear—still nonchalant, drawing the branches to its mouth and skilfully stripping the berries off
with its teeth. I am reminded of the Gary Larson "Far Side" car-
toon in which two bears are secretly watching a nerdy couple pic-
nicking, and one says to the other: "C'mon! Look at these fangs!
Look at these claws! You think we're supposed to eat just honey
and berries?" At a distance of fifteen metres, I cannot help but
realize that I would make a better meal than those berries.

It is time. I take careful aim. And fire. A discernible orange cloud
shoots across the landscape...but stops just short of the target. A
light wind intervenes, scoops up the cloud and pushes it towards
an open window at the back of the fish plant. At first there is
silence. Bob and I are still checking for reaction from the bear.
Then, the fish plant door hastily opens, and Billy Larsen stumbles
out, coughing and gasping for water. I am quick to apologize, and
he responds with typical native stoicism: "It works. That's for sure."
As for the bear, it doesn't even look up. As it shuffles off upstream
to look for more berries, I am left to conclude that, on this day at
least, I am the most dangerous creature in the forest.

Mining giant Cominco employs a hovercraft, once used to transport tourists in Australia, to haul gold ore between the Alaskan community of Wrangell and the underground Snip mine on the Iskut River in British Columbia's Golden Triangle. (Larry Pynn)

3

THE NEW GOLDFIELDS

My ride has arrived. The *Hover Freighter*, a hovercraft owned by mining giant Cominco, is poised over the middle of the Stikine River, propellers churning wildly and water spraying out the back with hurricane force. Wrapped in a black rubber cushion, radar unit swirling, its big white air vents protruding from the deck like flared nostrils, the hovercraft is an intimidating sea monster with a ravenous appetite of up to 340 litres of fuel an hour. I can hardly keep it waiting. Bob and I hurry down the bank of the fish camp to one of his fish boats and motor out to confront the snarling, synthetic beast. As he carefully pulls alongside the hovercraft's port side, I scramble up the cushion with my duffel bag and onto the deck, the gale tearing at my hair as I make my way to the second-storey control cabin. Simultaneously, the hovercraft surges forward up the mysterious Iskut River, the largest tributary of the Stikine, leaving Bob in a spray of fine glacial mist.

The Iskut is a brief diversion for me, not officially part of the all-Canadian Stikine route, but nonetheless exercising great significance in the annals of Canadian gold-rush history. The first miner known to have attempted exploration of the Iskut was Alexandre (Buck) Choquette, a swashbuckling French-Canadian miner who'd cut his prospecting teeth during the California gold rush of 1849 and Cariboo rush of 1860. His canoeing party of Tlingit Indians in 1861 refused to accompany him up the Iskut for fear of encountering a fierce tribe responsible for past massacres of their people. Choquette had no option but to continue searching farther up the Stikine, successfully striking gold at a spot on the river that became known as Buck's Bar, near Glenora.

When Choquette sailed into Victoria harbour aboard the schooner *Nonpareil* in January 1862 with a pouch full of gold and a pocketful of embellished stories about the Stikine's gold-bearing potential, he touched off the first, if short-lived, gold rush in this part of the world. From that point on, Choquette's fate would be inextricably linked to mining and fur trading in Canada's northwest as either a prospector, a businessman or a representative of the Hudson's Bay Company. He held a favoured position among the Tlinglit people, too, as the husband of Georgina, daughter of the Chief Shakes of that era, and he worked with the Victoria *Colonist* to discourage north-bound miners from trading whisky with the natives. In 1881, twenty years after his first attempt to explore the Iskut River, Choquette returned to prospect the mysterious watershed but with no success. When news of the Klondike strike made its way out, Choquette, then seventy years old, took a steamer to St. Michael, near the mouth of the Yukon River on the Bering Sea, and transferred to a stern-wheeler for the trip upriver to Dawson. There he ran a store in 1898 at the height of the rush, and there he died, broken-hearted, a short time later at the news of the death of his son Henry in an accident at Five Finger Rapids on the Yukon River. Although Choquette's exploits are virtually unknown among Canadians, enjoying none of the fame of, say, gold miner Billy Barker or explorer Simon Fraser, cartographers have at least enshrined his name in a series of landmarks—a mountain, a glacier and a tributary river—along the lower Stikine River near the Iskut.

If it isn't Klondike history, then what lures me up the Iskut River, this major stream on the Stikine's 550-kilometre journey from the Cassiar Mountains to tide water? A modern-day gold rush, unlike any other in these parts, erupted in the later 1980s on the Iskut River in the Golden Triangle. The historic image of stalwart independent prospectors traipsing north to seek their fortune was gone forever, replaced by an army of engineers with helicopters and diamond drillers backed by multimillion-dollar corporate ventures. What is drawing me to the Iskut River this afternoon is Cominco's Snippaker Mountain gold property and the opportunity to see first hand just how far gold mining has progressed in the century or so since Choquette first canoed these waters.

But first, the journey aboard the *Hover Freighter*, the most unlikely means of transport ever to figure in a gold rush, aside, perhaps, from a few camels used as pack animals during the Cariboo gold rush. Inside the hovercraft's cabin, the door closed snugly behind me, I find a refuge of remarkable quiet and calm. Pilot Brian Leach at the helm and First Officer Bryan Sverre at his side are inspecting the river like mental minesweepers. While the mighty Stikine holds its own dangers for boaters, it is a Venetian canal compared with the shallow, twisting, log-cluttered waters of the Iskut. Seated four metres above the water surface, the crew needs every bit of height to survey their surroundings and prevent accidents. "We're not worried about the water depth because we can go overland," Brian says, unaware of the dangers that faced stern-wheeler navigation a century ago. "Sharp logs are what we're looking for. We go in and out and around them. Up here, you'll see thousands of them." To which his first officer tersely adds, "Millions. So many dead trees it looks like a war zone."

Right ahead is a particularly nasty stretch of water known as White Snag Pass. For Brian, who has worked as a hovercraft pilot in the Middle East, Australia, Taiwan, and throughout Europe, it's an irresistible chance to strut his stuff. "Normally we don't go through here. You can see all the logs. But I'll take you through." Slowing to sixteen knots, he meticulously threads his way through the debris, wary not only of possible punctures, which would slow the hovercraft, but also of wood being sucked into the props. Most of the flotsam is cottonwood, a shallow-rooted, valley-bottom tree that is the first to go in a high wind or following shoreline erosion. "Seventy percent is co-ordination and ability to assess in advance," continues Brian, a kid in a video arcade, operating the controls with his right hand, the throttle with his left. "You can see why we don't go through very often." There is no point in memorizing the terrain. The meandering, flood-prone Iskut River creates a new challenge each trip. Just the other day, the river was so congested that the crew had to get out with a chain saw and cut their way to freedom. "I've been doing this for twenty-two years," says Brian, who works a tiring twenty-one consecutive twelve-hour days, followed by fourteen days off. "This is the most difficult route I've ever operated on."

The hovercraft was built in Australia under British licence in 1987 for $5 million to serve the coastal tourist trade. It is twenty-five metres long and eleven metres wide with the cushion (eight metres without it). Powered by four 525-horsepower turbo-charged diesel engines, with two three-metre propellers, it is capable of fifty-eight knots but is today cruising at a comfortable forty-two. Each engine operates independently, allowing the craft to continue forward progress in the event of the breakdown of one. Built to carry up to seventy passengers, its original seating area has been ripped out to accommodate freight—in Cominco's case a precious cargo of almost 11,000 kilograms of gold ore concentrate, considered by Brian to be the first such assignment for a hovercraft. The one-way trip from the mine site to Wrangell is seventy-two nautical miles; it takes two hours and fifteen minutes, and the craft makes two round-trips a day.

Great Glacier fishermen view the hovercraft as an environmental disaster, claiming that it disrupts spawning salmon habitat and creates a wake substantial enough to erode the riverbank and make fishermen hang on for their lives. Cominco plays down their concerns, arguing that the hovercraft's impact is minor compared with the natural erosion and debris on the Iskut River and noting that using a hovercraft is far more environmentally friendly than punching an eighty-kilometre gravel road through the wilderness from Highway 37, the main route (to the east) linking central British Columbia with the remote Cassiar district. As Brian tells it, the craft makes less noise than a small outboard motor. Because the hovercraft rides on a cushion of air, relatively little engine noise actually penetrates below the water surface. "We're often in close proximity to seals," he says. "Not until we're within twenty-five yards do they swim away. For that reason, hovercraft are used for military minesweeping. They don't set off acoustic mines." To the company, the hovercraft is a modern mining icon that literally walks on water. "Cominco is the first company to use a hovercraft in this manner," Brian adds. "It has opened up this area."

Hoodoo Mountain, an ancient volcano on the Iskut River, watches a passing hovercraft, used to transport gold ore between Cominco's Snip underground mine and the Alaskan community of Wrangell in British Columbia's Golden Triangle. (Larry Pynn)

And what a region. To the north of us looms 2,000-metre-high Hoodoo Mountain, a fantastic cone-shaped volcano that erupted perhaps 20,000 to 100,000 years ago but continued to put out lava flows into the post-glacial period of the last 10,000 years. Hoodoo Mountain is part of a string of volcanoes known as the Stikine Belt extending from the town of Terrace in west-central British Columbia into Alaska. Although Hoodoo Mountain remains all but unknown because of its remote location, Canadian scientists believe it may be unique in the world, a phonolite volcano in which the magma erupted in large part beneath glacial ice. The results are startling— meltwater freefalling off the mountaintop's flat sheet of ice past steep cliffs dominated by 100-to-200-metre-high rock columns and herds of hardy snow-white mountain goats. Scientists cannot say whether Hoodoo Mountain is extinct or just dormant, but they do know there are lava flows just twenty kilometres away that are less than one hundred years old and that lava has undoubtedly altered the course of the Iskut River many times over the centuries. As the *Hover Freighter* skims past the volcano on its northern horizon, a tuft of white cloud hangs over the icefield like a blast of hot steam, suggesting that anything is still possible in this wild region.

Eventually, the 1,350-metre-long runway at Bronson Creek comes into view to our right—a strip of gravel, watered regularly to keep down dust, wedged between Cominco's Snip mine and Skyline Exploration's Johnny Mountain mine, an extensive operation that was built high in the alpine zone and operated until 1990, when waning gold deposits forced a shutdown. "Spot on 6 p.m.," remarks Brian, pulling onto the beach next to a flat-deck truck full of grey ore bags ready to be hoisted by crane onto the craft's cargo deck. A short walk up the side of the runway takes us to Cominco's modern mining camp, about as similar to camp conditions of a century ago as Leach's hovercraft is to a paddle wheeler. Home to 120 non-union workers, the camp is a two-level, motel-style structure with clean, carpeted hallways and well-equipped private rooms, each with a plush chair, telephone and desk, and all the conveniences of a country club. Miners can enjoy a weight room, a hot tub, a recreation room with pool tables, table soccer, juice and coffee, and—can you believe it?—a quaint, creek-side pub with satellite TV, fireplace, Sunday steak and hamburger barbecues and pints of draft for $2.50. Just another effort to make conditions as natural as possible, with the hope that a happy workforce is a productive workforce. But not too happy. At Snip, there are limits. The pub, operated by the Bronson Creek Social Club, closes at 10 p.m., and employees who abuse the privilege by becoming obnoxious or showing up at work under the influence are gone after two strikes. "Alcohol is a perennial problem in camps," explains mine personnel superintendent Garth Elsdon, who should consider himself lucky he doesn't have to deal with the sort of booze-'em-up camp conditions of a century ago. "But it's said there is no such thing as a dry camp unless you search everyone's luggage."

Whereas the old gold prospectors subsisted on rations of bacon and beans, this Cominco mess hall is wonderfully piggish. The cooks can pick out the newcomers to camp by the way they load up their plates with free grub. Only after a few days and a few unwanted pounds do they settle down and become more selective, more civilized. A typical breakfast offers bread, French toast, fried potatoes, pancakes, scrambled eggs, beans, ham, porridge, sausages, bacon, ten selections of cereals, four kinds of fruit. For dinner, you can choose from ribs, cutlets, turkey, beef, rice pilaf, brussels sprouts, wax beans, apple pie, Black Forest cake and pastries. The beef comes from Prince George, the chicken and pork are from Alberta, and it all costs $5,000 to $6,000 a week, not including freight.

The Snip mineral claims were explored intensively in 1986, with the facilities constructed in 1990 and the mining operation under way in early 1991. Cominco operates the underground mine on behalf of a joint venture with Prime Resources Group. Despite all the modern conveniences, staff turnover is 12 percent a year, and workers say every day at camp is a Monday, every day away a Friday. Miners work ten-hour shifts underground—twenty-eight days on, fourteen days off—earning $21.95 an hour for the first eight hours, time and a half for the next two. Over the year, they earn a basic $63,900. If you tack on holiday pay and profit-sharing bonuses, it's closer to $80,000. Many of Snip's miners were hired after closures at Cominco's Kimberley zinc mine in southeastern British Columbia. Others had worked the potash mines in Saskatchewan. And a few arrived from Skyline's Johnny Mountain mine over a seven-kilometre switchback gravel road after the operation closed in 1990. Every miner has his own reasons for working in these remote places, but they all involve money. Some miners are young, hoping to pay off a mortgage before moving back home. Some are older, and Snip is their last mine job. "We're careful about who we hire and we've been lucky," Garth says. "Our people are first class. A lot of them have a minimum ten years' experience."

The morning after my arrival at Snip it is time to see for myself. Earl Masarsky, a mine geologist, leads me to a supply room where

The glaciated Coast Mountains form a spectacular background from the gravel road linking Cominco's Snip gold mine and Skyline's Johnny Mountain property in the Iskut River Valley. (Larry Pynn)

I am outfitted with an orange coverall suit, dark rubber boots and a white hard hat equipped with a battery-powered light. Then we jump into his orange Toyota Landcruiser and begin burrowing our way into the mine at Portal 180, situated at an elevation of 180 metres above sea level. Proceeding bumpily through the tunnels in a vehicle helps to ward off any symptoms of claustrophobia. The experience is not unlike driving a logging road at night (a practice, come to think of it, I would not recommend) except that the route is a freewheeling, 13-percent corkscrew grade rather than a series of switchbacks. "That big silly thing is a ventilation tube," Earl says with the efficiency of a Gray Line tour guide. "Blasting creates toxic gas. We have to dilute the air to the point it is no longer toxic."

Armed with a line of compressed air from the outside, the diamond drillers stick their needles deep into the earth's sedimentary flesh—eighty-one metres yesterday alone, a Snip mine record—to obtain core samples that will lead them on the search for the vein of gold ore. It is a finicky job. Drill operators closely monitor the gauges, careful not to exert too much pressure too fast that might jam or break the drill rods.

In case of an accident such as a fire, workers make their way to refuge stations, cave-like rooms with steel doors, concrete walls, an air supply and communications to the outside. "It's like its own world," Earl says. "You can't take anything for granted. It's something you develop in mining. Your senses become very acute." Maybe he's right. Right now, I sense I am growing whiskers. The dampness of the mine makes me feel like a water rat. Indeed, water seepage is a persistent problem, causing icy winter conditions in the five-metre-wide tunnels, making the rock unstable and forcing workers to bolster the fractures with steel bolts.

Amid all the blasting, drilling and removal of ore, the most dangerous job goes to so-called "raise" miners like Jan Chval, who precariously follow narrow veins of ore straight up through the rock, standing on spindly platforms. Miraculously, he has survived twenty-seven years in this business with a smile on his face. When I encounter Jan, he is at the end of his ladder, balanced on a wooden plank, face encrusted with mud. He is holding a percussion drill that is mounted on a telescopic swivel and operated much like a jackhammer, thrusting upward into a cubbyhole-sized, 1.5-by-2-metre passage. In the age of multimillion-dollar technology, Jan's raise setup seems precariously out of step, almost a medieval throwback to the bad old days of mining. But the fact is, this time-tested process is still the method of choice in small mines with narrow ore-vein passages. Some raises can stretch forty metres, and the distance becomes perilous.

When asked about the dangers, Jan turns his mind back to 1978, when he was working in Echo Bay's cobalt mine at Port Radium in the Northwest Territories. A plank in the staging broke, flipping him down a deep raise, tantamount to tumbling down a well. "I was bouncing off the walls, sliding down, upside down. I knocked myself out. When I woke up I found my knee ligaments torn. I flew to Yellowknife for surgery and spend three days in hospital and didn't work for three months."

The non-stop vibration of the drill has made Jan's hands wide and weary. And the dust poses a constant threat to his lungs. "Yes, this is quite a hard job," he concludes, "but I'm quite good at it. And I'm my own boss. Nobody looking over my shoulder." One

*Despite some dangerous accidents, Jan Chval keeps smiling after
27 years as an underground miner, most recently at Cominco's
Snip gold mine on the Iskut River.* (Larry Pynn)

thing's for sure: I will never again whine about having to string up outdoor Christmas lights.

After the shift change that afternoon, I seek out Jan in his room back at camp, where he is showered and relaxing with his friend, Alojz (it's so hard to pronounce, everyone calls him Louis) Pacalaj. Jan and Louis, both forty-eight, share an unusual story with me, a story that begins in the early 1960s in their native country, the then Czechoslovakia. Although they were born only fifteen kilometres apart in central Slovakia, the two miners did not know each other in their youth. Both worked the coal mines and both went to the same military training camp in the early 1960s before being assigned border-patrol duty in the Czech region. It was military policy in those days to have the different cultural groups guard each other's borders in the belief that they would not be swayed by ethnic loyalties if trouble broke out. Under those circumstances, there was no love lost between the local citizenry and the uniformed border guards, who were given the disparaging nickname "watermelons"—green on the outside, red on the inside. Both miners would eventually escape from Czechoslovakia. Louis took off one night in 1968, crossing into Austria with his dog and machine gun. Jan's ticket out came seven years later. He had returned to the coal mines and in 1975 received a free bus ticket for a holiday in Yugoslavia, a reward for record production in the mine. While there, he crossed the border into Italy and never went back.

Both men eventually immigrated to Canada, where they sought employment in the mines and ended up at Johnny Mountain. The first time they met in the mine's recreation room, they knew they'd seen each other before, but couldn't put a finger on where. Gradually, each backtracked through his life and returned to those days in the military training camp. "Then it struck me; he was the tall guy right in front and I was the short guy in the back," Jan confirms. "When he was younger, he was skinny and tall and his helmet was standing up just like a mushroom. That is something you don't forget."

Today, despite the high wages, good benefits and modern amenities, the two men have not forgotten the tough times, the hungry times. This is Louis's first camp with a telephone in his room. "It's very good," he says, holding out a $50.45 phone bill showing a forty-one-minute call to Czechoslovakia. And you can still find him going into the mines carrying four veal cutlets wrapped in a napkin. Just in case. To him, even cutting the fat off a pork chop doesn't sit right. "I was skinny and never had enough to eat. I feel guilty throwing food away."

Only a third of Snip's employees actually work in the mine. The rest handle a variety of jobs, including the office, yard, warehouse and assay office as well as the shop, mill and hovercraft maintenance. The operation of such a big facility without roads and so far from civilization generates special problems. "It's not like you can snap your fingers and get service across the street," confirms the warehouse supervisor, Jack Hill. He oversees a $1.9-million inventory of 7,000 items—from drill bits to boots, gaskets to air valves, oil to cement, dynamite to work pants—supplied by 600 industrial vendors around North America. "We go through a lot of tires," he adds. "Get a sharp rock and it tears the heck out of them."

Eighty percent of the stock is barged up the Inside Passage to

Wrangell, the other 20 percent, much of it from the United States, is flown in via Smithers, the nearest sizeable British Columbia town, at sixty-five cents a pound. Of course, when weather in the Coast Mountains makes flying impossible it's another matter. "There's been some pretty hairy moments," concedes Bill Wilhite, the maintenance foreman. "We've done some pretty weird things to get us over a couple of days, mostly trying to jerry-rig things, making components usable." In preparation for winter, the warehouse stocks up like a red squirrel, ordering enough parts to carry the mine through the next few months. "We break most anything, but hydraulic hoses take up a lot of our time," Bill says. As we speak, mechanic Greg McDonald walks up with bad news. "The solenoid is fried and we don't have another in stock. It's fairly cooked, doesn't look good." The item, part of a truck starter, was ordered more than a month ago. "Some suppliers are good," says Bill. "To others, it's not particularly important to them. We'll try to repair the old starter."

The mine's mill uses a gravity-flotation system for recovering the gold, which is less efficient than a cyanide process but poses less risk to the salmon-rich Iskut River. The mined rock is fed through a primary jaw crusher, then through a secondary cone crusher, then pulverized by forty tonnes of small steel balls. Water is added to form a slurry, and the gold is separated from the ore on a water-fed mineral jig and a shaking table—a sophisticated two-step version of the gold pan, in which gravity pulls down the heavy gold and separates it from the waste rock. From an estimated 450 tonnes of rock mined every day, the company extracts 91 percent of the

A twin-engine Douglas DC-3 takes off from a dusty gravel airstrip, delivering gold ore between Cominco's Snip mine on the Iskut River and the Alaskan port of Wrangell. (Larry Pynn)

gold—an average of 11,500 troy ounces a month—one-third on site from the coarser gold, two-thirds from fine concentrate shipped to Japan for final processing. The other 9 percent is lost to a mine tailings pond two kilometres away that is seasonally decanted into Monsoon Creek, a tributary of the Iskut River. To date, there have been no noticeable environmental effects and none of the problems of acid drainage (sulphuric acid, created when mined rock is exposed to the air) encountered in some other gold mines. At the current rate of production, and in the absence of new ore discoveries, the mine is expected to run out of gold by 1998. "It's about one ounce per tonne," says Kieran Loughran, the mill foreman. "One of the highest production mines in Canada. Very profitable for the company."

On my final day at Snip mine, awaiting transport back to Great Glacier by hovercraft, I stand beside the runway taking photographs of the loading of long rows of ore-concentrate bags into a Douglas DC-3 aircraft. I laugh when one of the pilots pulls his pants down and moons me from the cargo door. How typical of the North. I cannot help but wonder: Are eccentric people attracted to these remote realms, or does the landscape mould them after they arrive, allowing them the freedom to be themselves? As in all matters, the truth must lie somewhere in between. Minutes later, the Central Mountain Air DC-3 fires up its twin engines, sending a spectacular cloud of dust skyward as it speeds down the runway. No sooner is the aircraft airborne than the pilot banks sharply over the Iskut River and comes back toward the runway, low overhead, before climbing sharply over a palisade of mountains.

I smile, nervously this time. In the mad corporate dash to the Golden Triangle—at one point, more than a dozen companies were using the Bronson Creek airstrip—pilots and their aircraft have paid a heavy price, dropping out of the sky at an alarming rate over the past five years. It is almost as though the fears expressed by the Tlingit Indians to Buck Choquette about the Iskut River are as valid today as in 1861.

Cominco describes the flying conditions as "uniquely hostile." Indeed, conditions in northwestern British Columbia are among the most dangerous in the world. The temperate Pacific Ocean and the 3,000-metre-high Coast Mountains make an unruly partnership. The weather is unsettled and unpredictable year-round but particularly in winter, when low fog becomes so thick mine workers cannot see across the runway. At the same time, the rugged, unforgiving topography gives aircraft crew and passengers little hope of walking away from a crash. And to top it off, northern pilots may be a young and less-experienced lot, they are flying ageing aircraft, and the pressures of working long hours under difficult conditions may prompt them to take chances.

The Golden Triangle jinx started fairly innocently in June 1987 when a Diamond Aviation Norseman aircraft landed on the soft gravel runway at Bronson Creek. The left wheel and axle separated from the landing-gear strut, and the plane nosed over, causing one injury. Then, a year later, the main rotor of a Bell 206B Jet Ranger belonging to Northern Mountain Helicopters, flying from Bronson Creek to Sky Creek on Johnny Mountain, struck a tree in a mixture of fog, wind and rain, killing the pilot and passenger. One night earlier, the pilot had telephoned his father and reported that he was tired and "boy, they're really pushing us here." He'd worked nineteen consecutive days before the day of the accident and had drawn two thirteen-hour shifts in the preceding two days. Northern Mountain had obtained Transport Canada permission to increase his flying time to 450 hours from 300 hours in a ninety-day period. The pilot signed the letter requesting the change and told the maintenance engineer he was happy to get the extra work.

In the summer of 1988, a Trans-Provincial Airlines Bristol Freighter, a bulbous, Second-World-War relic, was carrying a cargo of 1,600 U.S. gallons of jet fuel from Wrangell to Bronson Creek. While landing, the aircraft drifted toward the right side of the runway, and one wheel ran off the edge. As the pilot attempted to correct the problem, the plane veered sharply and went off the left side, collapsing both main landing-gear struts and splitting the fuselage from nose to tail. Somehow, no one was injured and the fuel did not explode. Then, in 1989, a Central Mountain Air DC-3 was hauling 1,054 U.S. gallons of diesel fuel when the right engine caught fire and quit. The pilot landed safely on the runway; the crew bailed out and watched as the burning aircraft rolled back down the sloping runway and off to the side.

In February 1990, disaster struck a fifth time—with a vengeance. Another Northern Mountain helicopter crashed during a crew-change flight between Wrangell and the Johnny Mountain gold mine, killing the flight engineer and five miners and injuring the pilot and a sixth miner. Because the crash occurred in Alaskan territory—on the frozen Stikine River just below Shakes Glacier—the U.S. National Transportation Safety Board investigated. The Washington-based agency's thick report didn't pull any punches, attributing the crash to the pilot's overconfidence (flying into known bad weather with only visual flight rules) and to pressure from the mining company to make the flight. According to the report, Skyline Exploration routinely chartered Northern Mountain helicopters for the weekly crew changes when bad weather grounded the fixed-wing aircraft. Even if nothing was said directly, the subtle pressure was there: from the company, which wanted a fresh crew in the mines, and from the weary miners completing their rotation and looking forward to flying home. As the pilot, Robert F. James, told investigators, Skyline viewed the chopper as just another piece of mining equipment. "Throw the boys in the helicopter and take them home," was the prevailing attitude, as though flying in poor weather conditions was no more dangerous than driving a pickup in snow. It would take greater courage for a junior pilot to say no to that kind of pressure than it would for a veteran like Bob Curispon, a chopper pilot with twenty-three years' experience and 15,000 flying hours. He told crash investigators of working a two-month shift at the Johnny Mountain mine in 1987 and vowing never to return. "When you first go onto that mountain you instantly realize that you are into something like a third-world country," he stated. "Human life has absolutely no value to them up there. Fifty feet of visibility is considered a good flying day by them, and you are supposed to be out there and doing everything under those kinds of conditions. The helicopter at that time was a Bell 206 and we have a HF (high frequency) antenna sticking out the nose of it. They kind of thought that HF antenna was a curb feeler, feeling your way up and down the side of the mountain and you were expected to use it. They were continuously pushing...."

Just six months after that devastating crash, the pilot of a Bell 206B helicopter owned by Trans-North Turbo Air was returning to base in late summer after dropping off a work crew in light rain and wet snow. As he entered a mountain pass, he slowed almost to a stop, allowing snow to accumulate on his wind screen. Sucked into a downdraft, the pilot misjudged his rate of descent, hit the ground prematurely and the helicopter rolled onto its side. He escaped with injuries. Then, in 1991, there was yet another Northern Mountain accident, albeit a minor one. A pilot unloaded some day-shift drillers and was about to take off from a snow-covered log pad when the chopper skidded, its tail rotor hit the ground, and its skids slipped between the logs. Again, the pilot walked away with injuries.

That's it. Seven accidents, eight deaths and ten injuries in less than four years. Considering them individually, you might conclude the accidents to be an unfortunate aspect of the risky business of commercial flying in extreme northern conditions. Together, however, they make up a series of tragic events that raises many questions about mining-company charter flights in this remote region called the Golden Triangle.

As I stand in the dusty wash of the DC-3 droning out of sight over Johnny Mountain, I silently pray that the mountain gods will be gentle with the brave souls who risk so much for the commerce of the North. I pray that the jinx is over, that the aircraft parts littering the border of the airstrip—a wing from the crashed Bristol Freighter, the tail section from the burned DC-3—are just footnotes to history, relics of the bad old days of bush flying. But my prayers would go unanswered. Just five months after my departure from Bronson Creek, another Central Mountain Air DC-3 crashed, killing both crewmen. Only two minutes after takeoff from the runway, the plane stalled in strong winter winds, rolled sharply to its left and smashed into a horrific tangle of metal on a frozen gravel bar in the Iskut River, just a few paces from where I now stood. The cause could not be determined, but federal investigators discovered that the plane's 2,700-kilogram cargo had been loaded in a way that was contrary to aircraft recommendations. The cargo, of course, was gold ore.

With the Coast Mountains as a backdrop, members of Great Glacier Salmon Co-op driftnet fish on the lower Stikine River, just inside the British Columbia border with Alaska. (Larry Pynn)

4

TO THE VALLEY OF GOLD

Bill Sampson is the top of the food chain in these parts. In summer, he fishes for Great Glacier Salmon. In winter, he works a trapline. And pretty much any time of year when he needs fresh game he goes into the bush and shoots it. Just like that. Sometimes he seems part animal, too: fiercely determined, a little unpredictable, best not tangled with. He says he prefers to mind his own business, but he also likes to speak his mind. Except about himself; there is precious little he has to say on that subject. Maybe it's a survivalist thing: don't give someone ammunition that might one day be used against you. What he's willing to reveal is that he is forty and grew up in the Okanagan Valley at Penticton. He got his first taste of the wilderness as a teenager during fall hunting trips with his father to the Interior mill town of Prince George. After graduating from high school, he went to the University of British Columbia in Vancouver for his Bachelor's degree. But the only thing he figures he really has to show for all that education is his wife, Ruth. Together they moved north and squatted on a remote stretch of the Stikine

River, just downstream from Glenora and accessible only by air or boat. They have two boys, Myles, ten, and Russell, five, and a big, furry "Northern bastard" dog named Patch. The family works hard because, as Bill puts it, when you stop pushing in the bush, nothing happens. If he has a philosophy, it is this: When it stops hurting, you die.

Commercial fisherman Bill Sampson motors through the Little Canyon of the Stikine, one of the tougher spots for stern-wheelers heading upriver to Glenora and Telegraph Creek during the Klondike gold rush. (Larry Pynn)

And when it comes to making my way up the Stikine River to Glenora and Telegraph Creek on the next leg of my journey, I couldn't ask for a better guide. Bill leaves nothing to chance: a spare outboard motor on his five-metre, flat-bottomed aluminum skiff in case of breakdown, a Mustang floater suit for warmth and buoyancy in case we capsize, ear guards to protect his hearing during the day long journey. Signs, too, of a frugal man. He doesn't own a comb or a watch. And I suspect the only reason he has for not replacing his missing front tooth is that he can eat moose meat just fine without it.

More important from my perspective, Bill is familiar with the river—its rich gold-rush history and its flaws of character that can make it so dangerous. Normally the trip from Wrangell to Telegraph Creek, head of navigation on the Stikine, takes six hours. But Bill recalls the time it took him seven hours just to reach Great Glacier, fighting fifty-knot headwinds in winter. Spring and early summer can be just as dangerous, when meltwater from the glaciers swells the river to frightful proportions. "I've rescued three parties of canoeists and kayakers so far this year," he says, packing his gear into the boat. "They get halfway down the river and find they've overstepped their bounds. They just pull over and say, 'I'm not going farther.' I respect them. When the river is high, the velocity is probably fifteen knots. The hazard is the sheer between the currents and the back-eddies and the whirlpools. Plus it's wall-to-wall with sticks and trees and brush."

Bill fires up the fifty-horsepower outboard motor and pulls away from the dock, manoeuvring around a handful of small icebergs that have calved off the Great Glacier and are floating downriver. Russell comes with us while Ruth and Myles continue fishing in another boat farther downstream near the salmon camp. Out on the river the wind is brisk and cold, the weather brooding and unsettled. Low cloud hangs on the mountain tops, waterfalls hemorrhage down the steep slopes, chunks of ice sit wedged in the rock cliffs like creamy white fillings, and, to our right, the Choquette River enters the Stikine, cold and milky from glacial runoff. The landmark is an excuse for Bill to speak his mind. As far as he's concerned, Buck Choquette's discovery on the Stikine in 1861 was just the first in a long line of gold scams that continue to this day. "Maybe I'm too big a cynic," he concedes. "But they found a little gold, some miners came up, they sold them a bunch of stuff and got the first riverboats to start coming."

Although close to sixty commercial riverboats chugged and bumped their way up the Stikine between 1862 and 1969, it was the stern-wheeler that dominated the three gold rushes ending in the Klondike stampede of 1898. With a flat bottom and shallow draft, this vessel was well suited to the shallow river. The stern paddle wheel also had the option of going in reverse to free the bow from gravel bars. But the stern-wheeler had limitations, too. Vessels that became stuck heading downriver in fall when the water levels were dropping risked being frozen in and crushed to bits by the next spring's ice floes. Equally important, stern-wheelers were not all created equal. Some of the stronger vessels with experienced captains (as knowledgeable as you could get, given the infancy of exploration on the Stikine and its myriad of ever-changing channels) might plough upriver from Wrangell to Glenora and Telegraph Creek in two days. Others took a week or more and were consid-

With their flat-bottomed construction, stern-wheelers such as the
S.S. Strathcona, *shown unloading supplies on the beach at*
Telegraph Creek, could travel in shallow water. (B.C. Archives
and Records Service)

ered lucky to get there at all. Faith Fenton, the Toronto *Globe* correspondent, described one steamer that took eight days to reach
Glenora, "where she arrived with a thoroughly frightened lot of
passengers who had, at various times, leaped into the water, jumped
to the nearest rocks, sat with life-preservers fastened waiting for the
boat to go to pieces and spent dreadful hours when the boiler—an
old one—panting under the undue pressure of steam, threatened
an explosion."

Where the river ran fastest, steel rings were bolted into the
shoreline rock so that vessels could winch their way upstream.

Overnight, ships tied themselves to the shore with ropes and hung on tight. Vessels also risked collisions with rocks or wood snags and explosion of their overworked boilers. "In trying to avoid one of these floating logs, our pilot allowed the boat to swing broadside on and, the current catching her, dashed her into a pile of trees and driftwood, leaving a hole in her side 15 x 5 feet and below the water line," wrote Private Edward Lester of the Yukon Field Force. "Of course, the water rushed in and had we not had built-in compartments we must have sunk."

We proceed past a flock of Canada geese bobbing on the river like driftwood and then encounter a fork that Bill calls Amtrak, the Main and Broadway routes. Nipping closer to shore, he catches me admiring the stands of hemlock and Sitka spruce set back from the cottonwoods. Out among the living giants are plenty of notched stumps, too, evidence of the woodcutters employed to fuel the steamboats a century ago. "Each is a monument, each tells a story," he says, noting that the rush dried up so fast some men worked all winter cutting wood for which there was no market in spring. "I counted the rings once on a spruce: 230 years old." Since the early part of the century, when woodcutters logged the shoreline for steamboat fuel, the watershed of the lower Stikine and its tributaries has pretty much escaped the logger's chainsaw. But all that could change soon. Although the Alaskan portion of the river lies within the Stikine-LeConte Wilderness Area and the upper portions receive varying protection in Spatsizi Plateau Wilderness Park, Mount Edziza Provincial Park and the Stikine River Recreation Area, lower portions of the river remain vulnerable. The British Columbia Hydro and Power Authority has a long-standing proposal for flooding the eighty-kilometre-long Grand Canyon of the Stikine for electrical power, although it is unlikely to do so in the foreseeable future because of widespread public disapproval of large dams. Apart from ongoing mining in the Golden Triangle, the most immediate threat to the Stikine watershed comes, surprisingly, from the native people, those who should have the greatest interest in seeing it protected. Anxious to create jobs and give a kick-start to a local economic base, a faction of the Tahltan nation has teamed up with Interpac Forest Products, a British Columbia company, to seek provincial approval to log 300,000 cubic metres of wood annually in the Stikine watershed, including the Iskut River. It is a controversial plan, even within the Tahltan community, but it is also a clear sign that unless the government acts soon to save the Stikine watershed, industrial interests are poised to determine the river's future.

At Hope-in-Wall Mountain, Bill remarks that we are equidistant from his home and Wrangell, 120 kilometres each way as the river flows. "I've arrived at Hope-in-Wall in the spring to find eight feet of packed snow," he says matter-of-factly as we continue to wing our way upriver. Bill rides the edges of the exposed gravel bars as shallow as possible for maximum speed while avoiding the sweeper trees lying perpendicular to the riverbank. He suggests canoeists do the same but reminds them that in spring flood the gravel bars are covered with water and the Stikine is a river of death. "I pulled Bobby Ball's boat out of that slough," he says, referring to the guide-outfitter from Glenora. "It got caught in a log jam and just flipped over." What makes the Stikine so insidious is its speed and its blind channels, luring

71

boaters into a potentially dangerous tangle of logs. The debris is so bad that work crews are employed to cut down cottonwoods on the verge of collapsing into the river, leaving the stumps as a way of stabilizing the banks. Near the Anuk River, site of a former Hudson's Bay Company fur-trading post, we pass a group of kayakers and rafters. "This is a bad spot," Bill says, watching a devilish tree bob violently to the surface. "Nowhere to get off. I wouldn't want to be going downriver in that."

Since the first human wanderings in this remote and wild country, the Stikine River has posed limitless dangers to explorers, among them disease, malnutrition and freezing. But drowning, either by capsizing in the swift-flowing water or by falling through the winter ice, posed by far the greatest risk. If there was an innovative way to drown, both whites and Indians alike found it, falling through the ice in spring breakup, slipping off the stern-wheelers and flipping their canoes. Choquette's gold strike of 1861 prompted the Russian navy to send the corvette *Rynda* to the lower Stikine River in 1863 to investigate whether prospectors were mining on the Russian side of the river. Professor William P. Blake of California rode along as a scientific observer as the Russians paddled, poled and lined their way upriver on a gig, a sort of whaling vessel with a mast and sail. It was a strenuous trip and the crew almost capsized several times in the fast-flowing waters. Then, in the midst of negotiating a particularly dangerous rapid, one sailor was swept off his feet and drowned, cancelling any further exploration. It took eight days for the expedition to travel the 125 kilometres, including two and half hours to navigate the Little Canyon of the Stikine, and just seventeen and a half hours to paddle back downstream. On the final night's camp, the expedition's Tlingit guide ran away for fear he would be blamed for the sailor's death when they reached the *Rynda*, waiting off the Stikine delta.

The dangers of drowning are just as real for today's space-age traveller. Ahead on our left, the expressway sweep of the Flood Glacier through the Coast Mountains foretells more trouble. "This is Scatter Ass Flats," Bill says, switching to a new twenty-three-litre gas tank without stopping. "Shallows all over. It sure can be a pain in the ass. There is no apparent channel. You follow one and all of a sudden the water runs away on you and it's gone. With the flat light and clouds, I can't see anything." Taking another run at it, he adds, "Five years ago, this part was a raging torrent. A Catholic priest drowned—flipped in a canoe." It was a terrible accident. Father Andrew Allison of Whitehorse was among four priests travelling downriver in two canoes in July 1987 when one canoe capsized at about 9 a.m. One of the priests made it to safety on a log jam, but Allison and the canoe were sucked under. Over the next two weeks, officials conducted an extensive search by air and water on both sides of the river for twenty kilometres downstream. They found a few fragments of the canoe but could not find the priest's body. "The river used to come through a luge [run] into a cottonwood forest," Bill recalls. "Dangerous. Nowhere to go."

Ahead of us on the river, Bill indicates Beaver Point, site of one of the earliest shipping accidents on the Stikine. Built in Oregon in 1873 and measuring thirty-eight metres in length, the *Beaver* was a slow paddle wheeler that puttered back and forth between Portland and Astoria on the Columbia River. In 1876, the ship was sold to service the tail end of the Cassiar gold rush on the Stikine but just two years later ran aground and was wrecked. The owners salvaged the machinery but abandoned the rest to the river. "It sank somewhere downstream," Bill says.

Farther along, we see our first pine trees, evidence that we are gradually entering a drier climate in the rainshadow of the Coast Mountains. At a sandbar across from the Scud River and beneath Commander Mountain, Bill pulls ashore to chat with Vince and Lynne Murray, a school teacher and librarian from Moscow, Idaho, a university town near the Washington border. Having driven up Highway 37 to Dease Lake, then west to Telegraph Creek, the couple are in the second day of their canoe trip down the Stikine River. "It probably hasn't changed much in a hundred years," Vince says, eyes fixed on the frigid tongue of the Commander Mountain glacier. "Except there's fewer people." Indeed, this route to the Klondike is one of the few places in North America that is quieter and less populated today than it was a century ago. "This is a big river," he continues, discussing the Stikine's untapped potential for ecotourism, "but you'd better not advertise it too much or it will be shoulder-to-shoulder people, just like in Idaho." As Bill leads us back to his boat to resume our journey, he calmly concludes that the Stikine wilderness is one secret that cannot be kept from tourists. "They'll come anyway," he asserts.

Although we cannot see them from the river, high up the mountainsides lies a series of mysterious aboriginal stone cairns as tall as two metres. Perhaps demarcating some sort of tribal midpoint between Telegraph Creek and the Pacific Ocean, some of these cairns are also positioned with a commanding view of the Little Canyon of the Stikine, the next landmark awaiting us just upstream.

In 1887, George M. Dawson of the Geological Survey of Canada described the canyon as "three-fifths of a mile long and in places not more than fifty yards wide...bordered by massive granite cliffs, 200 to 300 feet in height, above which, on the west side, rugged mountain slopes rise." There are no rapids through the canyon, but the strong flow combined with the narrow passage were enough to have warranted special directional signals during the gold rush. Some travellers canoeing upstream during periods of high water had to wait for days until the river subsided to manageable levels. "They used to hang up a green ball or a red ball," says Bill, goosing his skiff through the surging passage. "That's where the term 'highball' comes from." A large wooden beam attached to a cable dangles from the right side of the upper canyon, the only visible evidence of the old flag station.

Guy Lawrence, who made his way up the Stikine aboard the forty-one-metre-long stern-wheeler *Skagit Chief* in 1898, recalled arriving at the canyon late in the day and having to tie up overnight in preparation for a daylight run. "At the break of day we headed out into midstream," he wrote. "The river here was rushing down in a torrent, fully two feet higher in the centre of the stream than on the walls of the canyon. With a great deal of puffing and snorting the steamer headed upstream. Ahead of us we could see a small point sticking out, and round this point the water really raced and foamed. Three times the captain tried to reach the point, but each time we failed. At last in desperation he left the wheelhouse and rushed below. Here he seized a spanner and applied it to the safety valve, then he rushed back to the wheelhouse swearing volubly. Once more we forged ahead and had almost reached the point when the dreaded cry "Man overboard!" greeted our ears. It was the unfortunate engineer, a very stout man, who had risked this form of death rather than being blown up by the boilers. We watched him receding down the river and finally observed him being swirled around in an eddy, where he finally seized an overhanging branch of a tree and hauled himself ashore."

For the next nine days the *Skagit Chief* remained tied up at the canyon while stronger vessels steamed past. To amuse themselves, the younger men would shinny along the bow rope to shore—until one fellow's feet slipped, his gumboots filled with water, and he was dragged to his death on the river bottom. Eventually, the *Stikine Chief* arrived to collect the stranded passengers, running the canyon in twenty minutes. After several more trips, the *Skagit Chief* was laid up when the crew filed claims against the company. The ship was sold in October the same year at a marshal's sale and taken back to Puget Sound. Despite the vessel's short stint on the Stikine, its name lives on at Skagit Chief Point, a protrusion of rocks where the steamboat damaged its rudder and ran aground.

Beyond Butterfly Creek, a distance of 215 kilometres from the sea, I am surprised to spot a lone harbour seal, doggedly pursuing the sockeye salmon on their spawning route to Tahltan Lake. Aside from a bald eagle, it is our only noteworthy sign of wildlife today on the Stikine. "I regularly spot bears swimming the river," Bill assures me; he has even damaged his prop by concentrating on them instead of the river flow. "Many times I could have shot a grizzly, but didn't. They're always great to see." Black bears aren't nearly so lucky. When Patch trees them, they are summarily executed as fur-bearers. Myles shot his first bear at age nine. "He can't work a computer, but he can tear a snowmobile apart," Bill adds.

We skip over a short riffle, pretentiously named Grand Rapids, and watch the Chutine River flow in from our left side. Bill remarks that he once found a boater up the Chutine, out of gas and thinking he was still on the Stikine en route to Telegraph Creek. Such is the sorcery of the Stikine. We are now only minutes from Pritchard Creek and Bill's homestead. It is already 8 p.m. and starting to get dark when we pull ashore at his property. "My legs are getting stiff," he concedes. "But it beats walkin' on the ice." Behind us, Russell is asleep, propped up against a gas drum. Bill shows me to his guest cabin and then hurries to the main house to start a fire and bake a fresh salmon.

He applied for his land after building a squatter's cabin on the site in 1974, but it was twelve years before he was allowed to buy eleven hectares, the start of his series of run-ins with Northern bureaucracy. "The biggest disaster is the government's failure to support settlement in the North," he says. "They are incapable of functioning outside their own plans. You don't need government planning to make a free-enterprise system happen." The family has a meat house for hanging moose and a workshop for building their own boats. "The little boats are safer," Bill says. "You can push, paddle and lift them off and they run on motors that you can pick up." He also owns a two-seater Aeronca Champ aircraft, powered by a sixty-five-horsepower motor, that allows him to keep tabs on what's happening in the surrounding region.

It is a comfortable homestead, but you won't find many of the modern luxuries. By choice. "I'd rather live beside a garbage dump than have a TV," Bill says. Sure, there are some things he cannot teach his kids. And it costs a bucketful of money just to motor upriver to get his mail. But he wouldn't change anything. "This beats anything else you could come up with. I have everything I want and more."

The next morning we are back on the river before noon, motoring through Dutch Charlie Riffle, past an abandoned native fishing site at Shakes Creek, and eventually pulling ashore near Brewery Creek on a long bench of land known as Hudson's Bay Flats. As Cottonwood Island was to the lower Stikine during the Klondike gold rush, so Hudson's Bay Flats was to the upper river. "This used to be a tent city," remarks Bill, stepping ashore. "Wall to wall for a mile, all the way up to Glenora."

At the peak of the gold rush in 1898, Glenora and Telegraph Creek bustled with some five thousand gold miners, lured by government promises of a narrow-gauge railway and a wagon road heading north to Teslin Lake. From there, it was a breeze of a boat ride down the Teslin and Yukon rivers to the goldfields at Dawson. That was the line being fed miners, but it turned out to be just another grand political promise that went unfulfilled.

The Yukon railway served as a national rallying cry at a time when the United States had a financial stranglehold on the Klondike gold rush. Not only were most of the miners American, taking any profits back home with them, but the United States also controlled access to the two busiest routes, the Chilkoot Trail and the White Pass, and held the lion's share of the coastal shipping and outfitting business. In a speech to the House of Commons in February 1898, Interior Minister Clifford Sifton boasted that an all-Canadian route would relax America's grip and allow Canada to take control of the Klondike by creating its own access over Canadian soil. As Sifton optimistically figured it, construction of the Yukon railway by the coming September (the cost to the contractors, William Mackenzie and Donald Mann, was conservatively estimated at $22,000 a mile of track) would reduce the time from Victoria to the Klondike to less than two weeks: three days by steamer to Wrangell, two days by stern-wheeler to Telegraph Creek, one day by train to Teslin Lake and seven days by boat to Dawson. "We are prepared to...prove that the route is a practicable route, and an all-Canadian route," he told Opposition Leader Sir Charles Tupper.

To prospectors, any route that could bypass the U.S. customs and both the rugged Chilkoot and White Pass trails out of Dyea and Skagway respectively sounded good. So to Glenora and Telegraph Creek they came, not just along the Stikine River but also, to a much lesser extent, overland through British Columbia's Interior on the Ashcroft Trail. In his book *The Trail of the Gold-Seekers*, the American author Hamlin Garland described arriving on the bank of the Stikine River in mid-summer of 1898 after fifty-eight wet and arduous days on the Ashcroft Trail. "Men were camped all along the bank, out of food like ourselves, and ragged and worn...." A total of 120 horses and 24 men eventually caught a ride across the swollen, fast-flowing Stikine aboard a steamer and landed at Glenora, which was already beginning to resemble a post-boom ghost town. "Instead of being the hustling, rushing gold camp we had expected to find, it came to light as a little town of tents and shanties, filled with men who had practically given up the Teslin Lake Route as a bad job. A couple of months before our arrival nearly 5,000 people had been camped on the river flat; but one disappointment had followed another, the government [rail] road had been abandoned, the pack trail had proved a menace and as a result the camp had thinned away and when we of the Long Trail began to drop into the town, Glenora contained less than 500 people, including tradesmen and mechanics."

The Yukon railway bill proved to be too controversial; not only would it have awarded Mackenzie and Mann the project without public tender but it would have given the contractors a limited monopoly over further railway construction in the region and awarded them a land grant of 3.75 million acres (based on 25,000 acres per mile of track over the 150-mile project) tax-free for ten years. The Canadian Senate found this too much to stomach and, despite protests from British Columbia, vetoed the project just as it was taking shape and just as the gold miners were pouring into Glenora. To a man and woman, the prospectors had been suckered in.

The disabused miners tried to fight back, but distance and poor communications made their actions futile. Politicians were even more isolated than they are today. In her dispatches to the *Globe*, Faith Fenton described watching almost two thousand men gather by the Stikine on June 10, 1898, three days after official word of the cancellation of the railway reached Glenora. The throng was already in an ugly mood after hearing that the postmaster, unable to cope with the deluge of mail arriving in the area, had burned much of it, a disaster for those who expected to receive forwarded money. Fenton reported that the gathering unanimously passed a resolution condemning the British Columbia and federal governments and urging that the stranded Klondikers be employed completing the wagon road. But no one acted on the advice. No help came. Although Telegraph Creek, as head of navigation on the river, survived as a modest community, Glenora's fate was sealed. "The little tent village by the Stikine is forlorn today," Fenton wrote; "...tents of discouraged miners are striking here and there, leaving ugly gaps in the long, curving, dusty roadway...." Glenora —the "Valley of Gold," whose name is a hybrid of the Gaelic "glen" and Spanish "oro"—had lost its lustre, degenerating into a wasteland of broken dreams and dashed hopes.

The greater number of these miners sold their provisions and returned home in disgust. For some, the heartbreak of failure and financial ruin in this alien world proved overwhelming. One German trekker hung himself from the crosstree of his tent here at Glenora, leaving a simple last request in a note in his pocket: "Bury me right here where I failed, here on the bank of the river." Some drowned in the rivers, fell through the ice or were knocked senseless by rock fall. Some spent the winter huddled in makeshift cabins, and some did not awaken to the warm promise of spring. "I touched a man's face, frozen solid," recalled Guy Lawrence upon inspecting the upper bunk in one such cabin in the waning days of the Klondike rush. "In the lower bunk I could just distinguish another face. Both men, of course, were dead. They had died of scurvy, neither one able to help the other." And other miners fell victim to gruesome murders—an axe hurled through a tent wall, a gunshot to the head. The opening paragraph of a story in the Victoria *Daily Colonist* headlined "The Stikine Murder" on April 27, 1898, reads: "A letter received on Sunday from a Victorian now in Telegraph Creek gives the facts of the murder of James Burns of Vancouver and J.C.

Clause of Chilliwack on the Stikine River, and also contains the information that Charles Erickson of Vancouver, who is suspected of the murder, cannot escape, being closely followed by the police."

Getting home when flat broke took a certain amount of ingenuity and good luck. Louis D. Taylor, a young native of Michigan who went on to serve a record eight terms as a colourful mayor of Vancouver, owned nothing more than a tent and two days of grub when he returned to Telegraph Creek and attempted to hitch a ride down the Stikine with the steamer *Duchesnay*. "She was named after the C.P.R. superintendent at Revelstoke, and I had in my possession a letter of recommendation from him. With this I tackled the captain. He told me I could sleep on deck that night and see him in the morning. Next day I saw him, he stood me a good breakfast, then showed me into a hold filled with baled hay." At Wrangell, Taylor sold his tent for five dollars and persuaded the purser of a southbound vessel to accept the amount as fare. When he arrived in Vancouver, his clothes were tattered and he had twenty-five cents to his name.

A century later, Hudson's Bay Flats is still a good place to pitch a tent and poke around for old ghosts. Bill drops me off where I can walk upstream and discover Glenora on my own terms. The raised rail bed, presumably created by some sort of steam shovel, is still discernible through the open pine forest. I walk slowly and savour every step, gorging on a bumper crop of Saskatoon berries and sidestepping fresh pancakes of bear scat. A hawk overhead shrieks at my passing, and a big cottonwood creaks with old age in the wind. I cross a rickety footbridge and climb up and over a bluff that offers an outstanding vantage of the river below. Along the way I spot the remains of a six-hole wood stove, some old barrels and a few garbage pits plugged with rusty tin cans and broken bottles. With a little imagination, I can almost smell the sardines and whisky.

Eventually I emerge on the riverbank next to a couple of modern cabins, evidence that a century later Glenora is down but not completely out. Eight families still live in the area on rural homesteads, an unlikely collection of Vietnam War draft dodgers, Pentecostal fundamentalists and earthy back-to-the-landers who haven't come up for air in a generation. But there are no stores and no visible townsite, the historic Hudson's Bay Company store having been moved upstream to Telegraph Creek to serve as the Stikine Riversong hotel, store and restaurant. Yet there is still some commerce to be found. On a tree next to the gravel road a sign reads, "Custom home baking, pies, bread, tarts. Flowers and hang baskets for sale. Garden produce." Journalists don't need an invitation to show up on your doorstep, but it's always nice to have one. I follow the arrow to Iron Road—no yellow bricks here—and enter Piedmont Farm, a forty-four hectare religious farming commune, first settled by Americans in the early 1970s.

Sure, some of the early settlers here were running from that crazy Asian war. But they were also concerned about a better life for themselves and their children. They pulled up stakes and headed for the promised land, impelled in part by the popular back-to-the-land movement. Why Glenora? Why so far from their roots? Well, it had more to do with geography than with divine influence. The mountains and the isolation provided a measure of protection, a spiritual shield of sorts against negative outside influences. But

*Kathy Syme, a member of a religious commune on the Stikine
River, shows why Glenora, located on the dry lee side of the Coast
Mountains, is famous for its agricultural productivity.* (Larry Pynn)

just a small measure. "You'd think it would be remote, at the end
of the road," muses Mark Stevens, an eighth-generation New
Englander who founded the commune and holds title to the land.
"One night we had twenty-seven uninvited guests for supper. That

was a record. Chile at one end of the table, New Zealand at the other. But I like geography. It keeps me up on world events."

Equally important to the homesteaders was Glenora's location on the dry, lee side of the Coast Mountains at a low elevation of about 335 metres—a unique microclimate conducive to farming with an average growing period of 153 days a year. Even to early European travellers on the Stikine River, the region's agricultural potential was well known. George M. Dawson predicted that "agriculture may before many years be successfully prosecuted, in conjunction with the natural development of the other resources of this great country."

Piedmont Farm is one small step toward the fruition of Dawson's dream. The commune sells both retail and wholesale produce as far afield as Dease Lake: in a typical year, 2,250 kilograms of potatoes, 675 kilograms each of broccoli and cabbage, 450 kilograms of carrots. Crops not normally associated with the North— zucchini, pumpkin, green beans—all grow naturally here without the help of greenhouses. The three families that comprise the commune derive a third of their farm income from vegetables, the other two-thirds from hay, eggs and flowers—dahlia, gladiolus, bachelor's button, baby's breath—five dollars and up for a small bouquet. A few of the members take odd jobs in the community, and Mark hauls freight to the Golden Bear gold mine outside Telegraph Creek. There is neither TV nor telephone nor electricity in the commune, although they do have a diesel generator and they recently installed running water and flush toilets. "It's been eighteen years since I lived somewhere with all the conveniences," says Kathy Syme, picking a handful of brilliant yellow calendula against the backdrop of Mount Glenora. "We lived on a trapline for three years. After that, Glenora was like downtown."

From Piedmont Farm it is a short walk down the road and up the hill to another homestead offering a sweeping view of the valley. When I knock on the door, the matriarch of the family, Lynne Thunderstorm—a self-described "New York Jew" who changed her named from Bernstein because "a thunderstorm is one of the most beautiful things"—shows up braless and barefoot and only too happy to talk with someone from the outside. You see, she is undergoing a bit of a crisis. No, it has nothing to do with her black right eye. If a domestic dispute is to blame for that, it involves the farm's rambunctious roving billy goat with the scimitar horns. He is experiencing his annual period of sexual arousal that includes unrestrained head butting and a unique talent for peeing on his own face. "You can take a picture if you want," she says. "I won't watch." No, Lynne's personal crisis goes much deeper than a superficial bruise. It cuts to the core of why she came here in the first place. Just two days ago, she abandoned her kerosene lamps and installed a waterwheel that generates enough electricity to ignite a light bulb. That's right, a light bulb. "It feels almost like an intrusion," she confides seriously. "This opens up a whole list of things. I feel very disturbed."

Lynne and her husband, Nava, came to Canada from New York in 1971 and spent ten years homesteading on the Wapiti River near Grande Prairie, Alberta. They eventually tired of the northern prairies and decided to fulfil a lifelong ambition to live in the mountains, in Glenora, to be exact. The couple are vegetarians, growing their own produce and raising goats, chickens and horses. Nava works at the Golden Bear gold mine—two weeks in, two weeks out—and Lynne operates a free walk-in store with toys, books and clothes. They have three children—Leaf, twenty-one, Raven, twelve, and Fox, five—and all are home-schooled. Leaf has just returned from two years of general arts studies at college in Grande Prairie. "It was culture shock," she recalls, sitting relaxed in the living room. "I'd never been in a classroom before and I found it hard working to someone else's time frame. I was really shy at first, but then I figured, these people don't know me, so I became more outgoing. Many of the students grew up on farms, but many were also city kids. They didn't think about food or basic living. They took everything for granted. Around home you also associate with different ages. But at college, no one associated with younger or older people. It was like living in a bubble."

Over the long term Leaf plans to become a veterinarian because this part of the world could surely use one. Unfortunately, her mother's dreams are not nearly so distinct. Glenora is not the place Lynne had expected. It's not that she misses New York. Urban cultural activities leave her empty, two movies leave her bored. Rather than sit through a concert, she would rather sing to herself or listen to the wind. The problem is that Glenora, despite being surrounded by an infinity of wilderness, can be claustrophobic. Downright cliquish. People fall into three groups, she explains. First there are her Glenora neighbours, the Fundamentalist born-again Christians with whom she has almost nothing in common. "They believe Satan is around every corner. Their kids can't listen to music or, heaven forbid, talk about boys." Secondly, there are the Tahltan Indians, who pretty much stick to themselves on their reserve in Telegraph Creek. And then there is the "partying group," who like to drink to make up for the social isolation. "I dreamed of a Zen-ish daily meditation and work routine," she reflects. "And I have experienced a level of peacefulness. But I also dreamed of friends, of a community so I wouldn't have to hide nine-tenths of my true self. In fact, I experienced a turnaround. I'm one of the few feminist women. I can't have the intimacy and honesty I'd hoped for."

5

THE FORK IN THE TRAIL

If Telegraph Creek were situated anywhere else, it would have been torn down, ploughed under and paved over long ago. With no special heritage protection, with more mice than people, and with the majority of its homes staggering like drunks, ready to fall on their faces at any moment, it is a miracle the village has withstood the ravages of time, much less the forces of bureaucracy.

Take old Howard Bradshaw's place. He is one of Alaska's founding senators, a self-proclaimed roughneck Democrat who bought his Telegraph Creek home in 1965 as a summer retreat and base camp for big-game hunting with his male friends. "I was chairman of Finance eight of my thirteen years in the Senate," he recalls with pride. "People voted with me or their town would suffer; they'd go through some hard times. It was a dirty business." Now retired and living in Denver, he returns to Telegraph Creek each summer as faithfully as the songbirds despite his creeping age and failing health: he is eighty-five, legally blind, and forced to feel his way through town with a wooden cane. What makes Howard's place

Howard Bradshaw, one of Alaska's original senators, faithfully returns to Telegraph Creek each summer despite failing health and the fact his neighbour's house, loosened from its foundations in a snow slide, is about to crash onto his own. (Larry Pynn)

so unusual is that a snowslide swept through the townsite, pushing the house above his right off its foundations and onto a small stand of trees separating the two properties. That was four years ago. And there the house remains, as precarious as a huge boulder teetering at a 45-degree angle. You'd think someone might have

In the years before the big Klondike strike, sleepy Telegraph Creek, located at the head of navigation on the Stikine River, served as a jumping-off point for prospecting inland in the Cassiar Mountains near Dease Lake. (B.C. Archives and Records Service)

done something about that by now, that somebody might have thought, "Hmm, if those spindly trees give way, old Howard's a goner. Maybe we should move that house." But no one did, and no one complained. Certainly not Howard. Not a blind man who's seen too much of life to be worried about getting squished by a

During completion of the Yukon telegraph line after the Klondike gold rush, workers used twenty-foot-high poles from the surrounding forest, galvanized wire from Great Britain, insulators from Quebec and oak brackets from Ontario. (B.C. Archives and Records Service)

In 1899, one year after the height of the Klondike gold rush, the Canadian government ordered completion of the Quesnel-to-Atlin gap in the Yukon telegraph line, a 3,000-kilometre link between Vancouver and Dawson. (B.C. Archives and Records Service)

house. That only happens in Kansas, not in Telegraph Creek. "I don't fear it at all," he confirms, pushing a shot glass of Hudson Bay whisky across the kitchen table at me. "I put a lot of credence in that old log cabin." Maybe Howard is right. Telegraph Creek doesn't need a facelift. It deserves its own time zone.

As place-names go, few have as circuitous a history as Telegraph Creek. The site was so named as a supply depot for Western Union, an American company engaged in an ambitious international race to complete a global telegraph link extending up the West Coast of the United States and Canada, through tiny communities such as Telegraph Creek, ultimately reaching Siberia. The project turned out to be an expensive and unproductive fiasco. A competitor successfully laid a telegraph cable under the Atlantic Ocean in 1866, forcing Western Union to cancel its overland megaproject. The construction crews hadn't even made it as far north as the Stikine River.

This had to be more than a little embarrassing to the inhabitants—there is something logically disturbing about a Telegraph Creek with no telegraph line. Someone, something, had to set the record straight, had to fulfil Telegraph Creek's destiny. That turned out be the Klondike gold rush, some thirty years later. The arrival of tens of thousands of would-be miners in the Yukon highlighted the need for improved communications with the outside world. Indeed, news of the big strike on Bonanza Creek was unbelievably slow getting out. Today, a few well-directed faxes would alert the world in minutes. But word of the August 1896 find trickled out so slowly it took the trekkers until the winter of 1897-98 to find their way north, a fact influenced equally by the speed of transportation. As correspondent Faith Fenton observed, "...changes

Sunday group photo of construction workers on the Yukon telegraph line through northern British Columbia, ordered completed by the Canadian government in 1899, one year after the height of the Klondike gold rush. (B.C. Archives and Records Service)

occur with greater rapidity than our present slow system of communication with the outside world can record. If it were possible to overtake copy on its journey eastward, much of it would be killed by the correspondent who, at the time of writing, was expressing the exact truth."

Faced with this information vacuum, the Canadian government, in December 1899, authorized the Dominion Telegraph and Signal Service, a branch of the Department of Public Works, to

Galvanized telegraph wire being unloaded at Camp Rochester on the shores of the Stikine River near Telegraph Creek, Mile 0 on the Teslin Trail to the Klondike. (B.C. Archives and Records Service)

complete the Quesnel-to-Atlin gap in the Yukon telegraph line, a 3,000-kilometre link between Vancouver and Dawson that by its routing assured Telegraph Creek's continuing role as the only population centre on the Stikine River.

But the Yukon telegraph proved to be a controversial proposition, fraught with delays caused by weather and supply problems and a budget that ballooned from an original estimate of $225,000 to $420,000 by March 1901. The twenty-foot-high telegraph poles were cut from the surrounding forest and spaced twenty-four to the mile. The galvanized wire came from Great Britain, the insulators from Quebec, the oak brackets from Ontario and the workers' food supplies from Vancouver. When the line was finally finished in September 1901, William Ogilvie, Commissioner of the Yukon, sent out the first message: "Time and space annihilated. We are of the world now." Ironically, by the time construction was completed, both the gold rush and the population of the Yukon had already starting to ebb, lessening the need for a telegraph line. Heavy snows and persistent deadfalls in the region made for costly maintenance of six dollars a mile, about twice that of eastern Canada. All this combined with a diminished need for the line and abandonment was inevitable; it started in 1936 when spring floods wiped out major portions of the line between Hazelton and Telegraph Creek.

Yet only five years later, in 1941, Telegraph Creek was buzzing again, this time as a strategic transshipment point on a Second World War supply route. The Canadian government had awarded a contract for construction of an airfield at Watson Lake in the southern Yukon, part of a northwest staging route that would allow access to the North by air and eventually the delivery of American warplanes to the Russians to help the fight against the Nazis. With construction of the Alaska Highway still a year away, supplies for the airfield, including sand, oil, and asphalt, were shipped by the Barrington brothers of Wrangell up the Stikine River to Telegraph

Creek, then trucked overland on a rough road to Dease Lake, and finally delivered by boat down the Dease and Liard rivers.

As the head of navigation on the Stikine, Telegraph Creek owes its role in history as much to geological forces as to anything else. Just upstream from the community awaits the ragged, frothing maw of the Grand Canyon of the Stikine, a frighteningly beautiful stretch of landscape never boated in its entirety by a human. A handful of world-class kayakers have come close: so close that reports of their exploits say they "succeeded in navigating the length of the canyon." But their victory is only a technical one. A massive rockfall above the confluence of the Stikine and Tanzilla rivers has made negotiating one stretch of water so suicidal that kayakers portage around it. As Monty Bassett, a Smithers-based writer and amateur kayaker, puts it, "It is strewn with boulders and has a tremendous drop over a short distance. It's white water that has no green to it. No buoyancy whatsoever. It doesn't hold anything up. It takes everything right to the very bottom. It turns trees to splinters." You have to admire adventurous souls for giving it their best shot. After all, there is little left undone on this planet, as my own expedition shows. But from their failure I also derive the satisfaction of knowing that there are still some wild, unconquered places, and that the Stikine River is among them.

Getting to Telegraph Creek has never been easy. Not for the gold miners slogging away by dogsled, not for the stern-wheelers winching their way up river, not even for the modern traveller in the Winnebago. Despite increased mobility and improvements to Northern highways, Telegraph Creek in the 1990s is still as remote as it can get on a provincial highway in British Columbia. In fact, it is one of the few places where motorists would be better served by a topographical chart than a road map. From Vancouver, it's a good three-day drive, allowing time for gas and food stops and not much else. Motorists travel up Highway 1 to Cache Creek, north on Highway 97 through the Cariboo to Prince George, west on the Yellowhead Highway through the Bulkley Valley to the native village of Kitwanga, then north on Highway 37, better known as the Stewart-Cassiar Highway, to Dease Lake, the commercial and governmental hub of British Columbia's northwest Cassiar region. At this point, tourists take a closer look at their maps and the 120-kilometre dead-end gravel road running off to the west and decide to consult the self-described Bible of Northern Travel, the *Milepost* guidebook. "CAUTION," it warns, in big, bold letters. "Telegraph Creek Road has some steep narrow sections and several sets of steep switchbacks. It is not recommended for trailers or large RVs. Very slippery when wet. Watch for rocks and mud. There are no visitor facilities en route. DRIVE CAREFULLY!" It is at about this point that Ma and Pa Kettle look each other in the eye, think hard about their lovely grandchildren back home, and just keep on truckin' north to the safer motoring environment of the Yukon and the well-travelled Alaska Highway. Adventurous travellers, however, know the lure of a good dead-end road. Far from what the name implies, these routes are bristling with mystery, fertile habitats for exploration, a magnet for characters who shun the mainstream for the rewards of social and geographic isolation. Telegraph Creek will not disappoint.

When the Yukon Field Force marched through in June 1898 along with four members of the new Victorian Order of Nurses,

Lower Telegraph Creek, once the bustling stepping-off point for the all-Canadian Stikine route to the Klondike and later for the Yukon telegraph line, is a virtual ghost town today. (Larry Pynn)

created just a year earlier to provide health care in remote areas, Telegraph Creek was not nearly as bustling as Glenora. Private Edward Lester pegged the population at 350, including a large native population, and described the town as having two general stores, one hotel, two warehouses, a wharf, two bakeries, one restaurant, a dozen log homes and tents for the rest of the inhabitants. Delayed here while officials rounded up some three hundred horses for the journey north, the soldiers were anything but content. Heavy packs, punishing heat alternating with heavy rain, inconsistent rations, and mosquitoes so bad that smudge fires were occasionally lit inside tents to drive them out, all contributed to morale so bad it bordered on mutiny on at least one occasion. Lester noted in his diary, "They say we are to carry our large kit bags with all our belongings including our two double blankets and rubber sheet, the whole weighing seventy or eighty pounds. I can hardly believe this; are we soldiers or pack mules?" It can be no consolation to Lester a century later, but I reckon my own backpack weighs seventy pounds. The major difference is that I have no one to blame for it but myself.

Modern-day Telegraph Creek remains a living relic of the Klondike gold rush. Tourists are in fact excused for wanting to take the old village's pulse or giving it a gentle kick in the ribs for signs of life. The streets are laid out with the precision of gopher burrows, and there are no road signs. A few dozen houses, most of them empty and ramshackle, are arranged in a hodgepodge, terrace fashion. Among them are the one-member RCMP station with the big, cranky God-help-the-person-filing-a-complaint dog outside, the two churches, St. Theresa (Roman Catholic) and St. Aidan's (Anglican), still competing for a dwindling number of souls each Sunday, Howard's place, Melvin Callbreath's, and the home of Francis and Anne Gleason, a Tahltan couple who prefer to live off-reserve.

Francis has pretty much done it all: logging, mining, fishing, heavy-duty mechanics, trapping. Now much of his business is based on the tourist trade, repairing engine problems and conducting riverboat tours to Wrangell on his six-metre jet boat for $1,200.

The Hazel B No. 2, *operated by the Barrington Transportation Company, was typical of the diesel-driven commercial riverboats that operated between the Alaskan Port of Wrangell and Telegraph Creek, head of navigation of the Stikine River, in the mid-1900s.* (B.C. Archives and Records Service)

Sometimes he figures the river is all that hasn't changed in Telegraph Creek. Even the weather isn't the same. More snow these days. People come and go. Mostly go. And the riverboats are gone, maybe never to return. Francis's memory of river travel dates back only to the 1940s: not to the steam-driven stern-wheelers but to modernized craft such as the *Hazel B* in its various incarnations, commercial carriers with propellers driven by powerful diesel engines. "There was no road in here," he relates with a wistful look downriver. "Unless you flew to Atlin, the river was the only way out. They'd haul freight all summer by boat, and we wouldn't see fresh food again till spring." Tourists used to come on the river-boat, stay one or two days in town, then head back downriver. But with highway improvements to Dease Lake and easy access to the outside world, the number of riverboats dwindled. "My cousin, Edwin Callbreath, had the last riverboat, the *Margaret Rose*. It just faded out once the road came in. That was it for the river." In 1967 the *Margaret Rose* offered four-day, round-trip service between Wrangell and Telegraph Creek for $120 in heated cabins. It went out of regular service two years later.

That wasn't all that changed. With improved roads, Tahltan people could be found living anywhere in the province. Natives started to drink more. Social problems flourished. Even the leg-endary Tahltan bear dog, one of the few Canadian breeds, started a slow decline to extinction, presumably because it mated with other dogs from the outside but perhaps also for reasons we can-not comprehend. "It was a smart dog, with a different bark for every animal—moose, bear, grouse," says Francis, describing the dog as solid and fox-like, with sharp ears and a bushy tail. "When people started to take them out of here, to the Alaska Highway and Seattle, they all died. Nobody seems to know why."

One thing hasn't changed. The hub of the community is still

the historic Hudson's Bay Company store, now called the Stikine Riversong, a private store, café, lodge and gas station. The ambience of the café is country casual: get your own coffee, scrub your own table. The crowd is mixed: middle-aged tourists poking around for souvenirs, young adventurers gathering last-minute provisions for their trip down the Stikine and natives from the modern reserve community on the hill—Telegraph Creek's uptown, you might say. Accustomed to sharing in their large families, the natives are nonchalant about sitting down at your table if no others are available—something of a surprise to city slickers used to their own booth at Denny's—while their children lick the coffee spoons or the lids of those small containers of salad dressing. In season, old man Bradshaw holds court daily at his usual table, hands folded on his wooden cane, distinguishing old friends by their voices. "I understand you see women a lot better than men," challenges Bobbie Frederickson, the Riversong's buxom cook. "Yeah," Howard replies. "The nice thing about women is if you can't see them, you can still feel them." Be careful not to get him on a roll. "I must be getting senile," he laments deadpan. "When I go to wipe my bum, I pick my nose."

Built in 1898, the old Hudson's Bay Company building is the town's premier attraction, recognized, if not protected, as a historic building by the Heritage Trust of British Columbia. For the past fifteen years the wooden structure has been owned by partners Dan Pakula and David Fisher, expatriate Americans who settled here in the early 1970s. As white entrepreneurs dependent on native business but aware of simmering racial tensions in the community, the partners walk a fine line. They are careful to

Dan Pakula and David Fisher came north to Canada during the Vietnam era and now run Telegraph Creek's Riversong Hotel, a former Hudson's Bay Company store on the Stikine River.
(Larry Pynn)

stay out of Indian politics. They keep a low profile. And they are wary of journalists who might upset that fragile balance by reporting something that should not be reported. Sometimes I feel their reticence can border on paranoia. When I learn of a week-end reunion of some seventy past and present homesteaders in Glenora, Dan at first says I can come along. But overnight he has a change of heart, presumably after talking it over with others, and concludes my presence "would change the intent of the gathering." I fail to see how a wilderness writer in jeans and mackinaw would instil fear in these people, would somehow sour their lemonade. But Dan knows them best. Maybe they couldn't handle it. At any rate, there's no point arguing. His mind's made up.

David isn't any more interested in publicity than Dan, but when I tag along on a two-hour run into Dease Lake one morning, he doesn't have much choice. "I just do my own thing and keep on living," he explains, climbing steeply out of town over a spectacular route that parallels much of the Grand Canyon of the Stikine. "This is a world in which people have to get along. I deal with people as people." David has spent much of his adult life as a minority white, as a teacher first in the black ghettos of Detroit and later in predominantly native schools in small-town Northern British Columbia. Moving onto a plot of land east of Telegraph Creek in 1972, he lived simply the first few years with his wife, Tannis, from whom he has since been divorced. They grew their own food, moved about by dogsled in winter, hunted wild game. "It was a unique experience," he says, more than a little wistfully. "Everyone should see that view of the world." When the savings ran out, he moved south to Smithers to teach for a year, then returned to Telegraph Creek to take up Dan's offer of a partnership in the Stikine Riversong. David has done all right for himself, but you have to figure his philosophy must have changed somewhere along the way. The man who once lived in a fifty-dollar shack and shared roast moose head with natives around the campfire now resides in a modern log house with an outdoor hot tub and doles out supplies of marshmallows, taco chips, frozen pizza, and unleaded gas for the vehicle at seventy-six cents a litre. "I had no philosophy when I came here," he counters. "I knew that eventually I'd have to face the reality of making a living."

At 7 p.m. each day, the partners lock up the store and café and return to their homes in Glenora, leaving lodge guests alone to be entertained by the ghosts of the Klondikers until the next morning. My room overlooks the Stikine River, perfect for taking notes in the company of a bottle of 1988 Cabernet Sauvignon purchased in Dease Lake. From my window, the river is a silty, slate-green stallion galloping powerfully but silently to the Pacific. At dusk, the sky is slate grey and ethereal, and swallows descend upon the river like pieces of ticker tape tossed to the wind. Inside, everything about the place is old, even the reading material—a July 1979 *National Geographic* and a November 1985 *Science Digest*. The creaks in the floor are well aged too, and you have to wonder if the mice gnawing away at night are the town's last living descendants of the gold rush.

On the ensuing nights, I enjoy the company of Joan Sawicki, the first female Speaker of the British Columbia legislature, and her husband, Gary Runka, a land consultant and former chairman of the Agricultural Land Commission, the body created by the New Democrats in the early 1970s to protect farmland from rampant development. A man of integrity, he quit the post when Social Credit took over and ran roughshod over the commission's decisions. I had interviewed him several times over the phone for the Vancouver *Sun*, but we'd never met in person. He proves to be as down-to-earth as his background would suggest. "Have you been to the market garden?" he beams following a visit to the Glenora commune. "That's an impressive range of crops."

On another night I share the hotel with Danish photojournalist Anders Nielsen and his son, touring northern Canada in a rental van. He is anxious to talk about witnessing a most bizarre event— the auctioning off of the asbestos-mining town of Cassiar, a two-hour drive away to the north. He found the experience more than a little unsettling. In Europe, people don't do things like that. Towns are more than bricks and asphalt and glass and lumber. They are a cultural mirror, a historical statement, a commentary on the human condition. Oh, sure, they may wax and wane with the economic tides, but even a ghost town has much to say about life, about people. Cassiar opened in 1953 as the classic company town, tucked away so deep in the Cassiar Mountains that the community's 1,100 residents saw no direct sunlight between November and January. Not surprisingly, they were kept in the dark also about the closing of the mine right up to the last moment. During a visit to Cassiar six months earlier, I had found it to be a curious place filled with unusual people, like the good Catholic woman with fifteen children whose job, appropriately enough, was census taker for the federal government. When the mine closed, the residents moved on in search of other mining jobs. Everything that remained was sold. The sewage plant, copper wiring, heavy machinery, mobile homes, log houses, warehouses, cinema, fire hydrants, street lights, hydro poles—all went on the block. Anders had good reason to be disturbed. To sell the soul of a once-thriving community is more than distasteful; it is sacrilege. They even hawked the Anglican church.

In Telegraph Creek, too, the church is on the ropes. But the Catholics and Anglicans still duke it out each Sunday, keeping alive a century-old tradition of missionary work. A Presbyterian minister named John Pringle followed the gold seekers to Glenora and Telegraph Creek during the Klondike rush. Known for his boundless energy, fearlessness, cheerful disposition and honesty, Pringle went on to become a legend in missionary circles in the Yukon. He could work a team of sled dogs and in the absence of a church was quite prepared to deliver his sermons on the street from a beer-barrel soapbox. The modern church enjoys no such endearing status in the North. Church-run residential schools, in particular, are viewed as having disemboweled aboriginal culture, stealing children from their parents, cheating them of their language and culture and, on far too many occasions, leaving them emotionally scarred from years of physical and sexual abuse. It is within this historical atmosphere of alienation and mistrust that the modern Christian church must find its niche. Among mainstream Catholics and Anglicans it has produced a much humbler attitude, and it has shaped priests who are willing to listen and compromise as well as lecture.

I walk along the waterfront to the log church of St. Theresa and ask a hillbilly of an old man if the priest is around. "Well, I guess that's me," responds Father Denis Buliard, cinching up his belt, tucking in his shirt and passing a hand through his thinning hair. An emigrant from France in 1947, Buliard is now based in Iskut, a native community south of Dease Lake; he travels to Telegraph Creek to lead church services every two weeks. After twenty-six years of sowing seeds for the Lord in the area, he can count on just fifteen parishioners to appear for every sermon. "A lot of things have changed," he confirms in an accent as strong as aged cheese. "Life is changing for the native people, so it's bound to affect the church." Northern priests once held a close and strong relationship with their congregation, especially when they endured personal hardship travelling by dogsled to remote locations. With the advent of improved living conditions, ease of travel, materialistic attitudes and emphasis on native rights, that closeness has eroded. "The natives are going back to their own spirituality," Father Buliard quietly continues. "We try to adjust and adapt. There is no dividing line. Even their own leaders say there is no contradiction between the two. I agree to a great extent. When you come to a country like this, you have to reassess your own values."

A short walk down the street is Telegraph Creek's other religious bookend, St. Aidan's Anglican church, consecrated in 1924. I find minister Beth McClure outside in a floral print dress filling a water jug. Sunday church service begins in an hour, and she expects anywhere from twelve to twenty parishioners. Although her spiritual path to the Canadian wilderness could not be more different than Father Buliard's—she is a product of the Vancouver School of Theology at the University of British Columbia—her experience in the community has been much the same. "For many reasons, not the least of which was the church, these people have lost a lot of their culture, their traditions. They're struggling to recover them." Her role is to ensure that Christianity finds a place of relevancy along this uncertain path. "I did a Tahltan funeral this summer and it included some of the traditional ways. It was an experience for me. When a person dies, the children are hidden from the death scene. It's an evil spirit thing. During the funeral process, there are no children. They believe the spirit of the dead person might get into the children. Their understanding of death isn't wrong; it's just different. I have total acceptance from the natives. It's the whites that have a problem with it. They're not clear on the traditions. But we're working hard on how to bring native spirituality together with a Christian belief system."

One way to put Telegraph Creek into perspective is to walk past the Catholic church at the upper end of town, seek Father Buliard's gracious nod of approval, and then scramble on all fours up the dirt hill to the aboriginal cemetery, being careful not to roll any rocks back down into the parish. The view from here is as spiritually uplifting as you could hope to find. But there's more to it than that. What could be more appropriate as a headstone for this dying little town than a graveyard? Over the years, I've found you can learn as much about a community by strolling through such private places as by walking down the main street. The headstones speak volumes about the struggle for life. "In memory of Mary, a native woman, aged about thirty years, who met her death through the upsetting of a canoe in the Stikine River on July 20th, 1901." If you listen, you can also sense the silent cry of children buried long before their time, of lives measured in days, not months. "In Sacred Memory of Lancelot Creyke. Died Oct. 8, 1908. Aged 42 days."

Rather than return to the old village the way I came, I decide to walk along the crest of the hill through the reserve. Natives drive around in pickup trucks, passengers bouncing about in the back like sacks of potatoes. Those without wheels can call Willie Clem's taxi service, a small GMC pickup truck distinguished by a bumper

sticker on the driver's door that says: "Same shit, different day."
But I just keep walking on this day, past the drunken man shout-
ing at me from his cabin window and on to a big five-bedroom
white house with a wooden rail fence and a backdrop of pine trees
on the edge of a new subdivision. This is Three Sisters Haven, a
refuge for battered women named after a group of islands marking the Stikine River downstream of Telegraph Creek. I ring the
intercom buzzer, and administrator Alice Hamlin-Auger emerges,
apologetic that I cannot enter the facility. I am a man. This place
is as close as I'll get to a fort in this historic community: alarm system, electrically operated doors, RCMP on call twenty-four hours
a day along with four husky male volunteers from the reserve. "It's
secure," Alice agrees. "A lot of women in the community are not
afraid to come here."

Since Three Sisters opened (less than a year before my visit), it
has been a controversial issue in the community, a powerful statement about a lot of the unrevealed relationships between the gen-
ders in the North. "The men didn't accept it," Alice recalls of the
three-year struggle to establish the facility. "They made a lot of
jokes. Family violence and abuse had become a norm. But we say
to the abusers in the community that women won't take it any
more." With an annual budget of $250,000 a year, the haven has
enough staff to have a van pick up abused women and their families around the clock as far away as the Yukon border. A woman
stays for up to thirty days, then decides if she wants to relocate to
another community or return to her partner, who, with any luck,
has availed himself of counselling from Three Sisters. Indeed, the
weak link in the social chain is the lack of programs to help the

man deal with his problem. "Men thought we were going to break up families, but that's not our goal. We want them to stay together to heal, to become one. If the woman starts to heal, she can help her spouse along."

Alice's father was an American gold prospector, her mother a full-blooded Tahltan. As a youngster she lived in the lower village with the other whites and half-breed children, while the status Indians stayed uptown, on the ridge. Nonetheless, it was her mother's culture, not her father's, that she grew to adopt. That made returning to Telegraph Creek four years previously after a thirty-eight-year absence a lot easier.

The history of white influence on Northern natives over the past century is filled with heartache: the introduction of smallpox and other diseases for which the natives had no immunity, the stripping away of their language and culture to be replaced by alcohol and satellite dishes, the evidence of cultural degradation is all around. The language is almost extinct except among a few elders. There is too much drinking, too much family violence, not enough focus on the old ways. Two years earlier Alice made a personal statement when she married in a traditional ceremony, the first in recent memory on the reserve. She is a member of the Crow Clan, so her husband, a Cree, had to be adopted into the Wolf Clan. "The dancing, the feasting, the giving of gifts," she recalls with a warm smile. "I wanted to show the young people it's okay, it's a beautiful way."

But the chasm between natives and whites remains just as strong as before in the community. Like others in Telegraph Creek, she talks of the simmering resentment toward most of the

Fundamentalist Christians in Glenora—people who live apart from the Indians, who teach their children at home rather than send them to the reserve school, who follow a religion she can only describe as a cult. Yes, I hear her, but I have to wonder how closely her argument parallels the one used by white officialdom to trample native culture such a short time ago.

Walking back in the fading afternoon light, I manoeuvre down the steep winding road to the old village, pass a derelict car with a sleepy red fox as a hood ornament and inevitably wind up at Howard's place. Happy hour. Howard stopped drinking long ago, but he never gave up buying the booze. He dangles a whisky bottle like a social carrot, enticing passersby in for friendly conversation in an otherwise dry town. I am more than willing to play the game. Tomorrow begins the most challenging portion of my expedition—the overland trip by horseback and on foot some 250 kilometres north across the Stikine Plateau wilderness to Teslin Lake. I am anxious with anticipation and a little self-doubt—feelings not so different from those of the prospectors who took this route a century ago. I could use a good stiff drink.

Howard and his house are aging in tandem. Spider webs cover the kitchen window. The lawn grass is long and brown. The picket fence is weathered and falling down. And the branches of an apple tree are old and gnarled. He and three friends paid just $2,500 for the two-storey structure almost thirty years ago. It was their retreat, reserved exclusively for men. "We'd drink booze, play cards and eat moose meat," he recalls from his chair, hands draped over his cane. "No wives in this place. That was sacrilege." Memories of the old days are about all that draws Howard back every summer, experiences so vivid he cannot forget, even when he gets so old he cannot remember what he did yesterday. "This used to be a fun town, a jumpin' town. Hundreds of people. Trappers, guides, miners. It was a hot-blooded revolution." He revels in recollections of riverboat trips up the Stikine and having to winch the vessel through low water. Painful memories, too. Of the native woman who fell overboard and was drowned after a drinking spree on a riverboat run from Telegraph Creek to Wrangell. "Word went out, person overboard. It was midnight, pitch black, but they got that woman out and a doctor worked for hours with her and she never showed a sign of coming to. That was the worst incident on the river that year."

Yes, Telegraph Creek isn't the place it used to be. Much of the fun has gone out of the town. Young natives from the reserve regularly break into his home, and he keeps a couple of two-by-fours wedged across the back door for security. "I've had everything stolen—pots, dishes, silverware. I lost all my axes this year. My buckets. They tore my cooler to pieces. They busted up my broom. Malicious stuff. It's never ending. It's unbelievable." And if the kids aren't breaking in and taking over, it's the tourists. "A woman walked right in the other day while I was sitting at the kitchen table. She said, 'Sorry, I thought this was an abandoned house.'" Every year townsfolk figure this is Howard's last visit. After all, navigating the rickety boardwalks and winding streets of Telegraph Creek is a challenge for the fittest person. Howard has to be escorted around airports. He watches television with his nose pressed against the screen and even then only recognizes actors by their voices. But he can detect motion and continues to walk five kilometres a day, weather permitting. "I know you're wearing a wool shirt," he says, squinting forward across the kitchen table. "You've got curly hair. But I can't see your face. It's crazy."

Even a blind man can see what has happened to Telegraph Creek. What may appear quaint and funky to the outsider is a damned shame to Howard. "The Hudson's Bay store was everything. But the other night there wasn't a person in town. I liked it before. Where's everybody gone? It's kind of an eerie feeling. They must be all dead but me."

6

THE TESLIN TRAIL

Nobody else knows the Teslin Trail like Fletcher Day. For most of his sixty-one years, more recently as a big-game guide-outfitter, he has hiked and ridden horseback through this wild and remote quadrant of the Canadian North. Hell, as a young man he was earning seven dollars a day guiding the federal surveyors whose work is the basis for my 1949 topographic map. In those days he stood six feet, four inches—tall in the saddle even around these parts, where wilderness landscapes and the characters who roam them can assume unreal proportions. Although creeping age, three back operations and four bullet wounds from an irate ex-wife have cut him down a couple of notches, Fletcher is still a powerful presence. "It takes more than a shot in the head to kill a half-breed raised by the campfire," he says matter-of-factly. "Shoot a man in the legs if you don't want him to walk away."

Fletcher's knowledge of this land is the key to my further progress. Only he continues to stoke the flames of the Klondike rush, keeping alive the memory of the Teslin Trail, the route otherwise extinguished by the passage of time. His pilgrimage takes place over a few short weeks each summer. That's when he rounds up his string of packhorses, cinches their supply boxes down with a neat diamond hitch and moseys on north to establish his wilderness base camp prior to the arrival of wealthy big-game hunters from North America and Europe. Fletcher has agreed to guide me as far as the Koshin River, a six-day horseback ride away. Then he will head west to set up his fall hunting camp, and I will continue north, alone, on foot, to seek my own fate on the historic trail to Teslin Lake.

A century ago, the Yukon Field Force, the men who helped hack a crude trail through this landscape, began their tortuous overland journey to Teslin Lake at Telegraph Creek. But we begin on the banks of the Tahltan River, a fifty-kilometre drive northeast of Telegraph Creek over the Muddy Lake Road, a stretch of gravel leading to the Golden Bear gold mine. Public access to the road is restricted to protect this wildlife-rich area from overhunting, but Tahltans work the mine and grade the road under contract, a reflection of the band's decision to support development in their traditional area, as long as they get a slice of the action. "The Tahltan believe in development," confirms Fletcher, who operates a grader when he's not guiding hunters. "We work with industry for jobs and better economic conditions despite criticism from Indians in southern B.C. Development is going to come anyway. You might as well be a part of it."

We arrive at the Tahltan River in a dust-covered convoy of horse trailers and pickup trucks filled with Fletcher's relatives. The gear is unloaded, the horses are hobbled to prevent them from straying too far, and tents are set up for our first night. A couple of hours

Guide-outfitter Fletcher Day and his daughter Amy allow their horses a drink on the Koshin River during a wilderness horseback trip on the old Teslin Trail on the Stikine Plateau. (Larry Pynn)

later, the band of well-wishers finish their beer, shake our hands and drive back down the road to Telegraph Creek. When the last particles of dust have settled against the evening sun, five of us remain, an eclectic mix of cowboys, Indians and city slickers.

Skilled with horses and the ways of the bush, Day's daughter, Amy, the sixth of ten children, was raised in Telegraph Creek at her daddy's campfire. When she was old enough, she tagged along on the fall hunts, cooking and helping out. Then, during a big-game hunt a decade ago, one of Fletcher's clients exceeded his bag limit: he fell in love with Amy and took her back to Milwaukee, of all places, to work in a delicatessen. But beer and baseball games are no substitute for the Canadian wilderness. Like a salmon returning to the place of its birth in the fall, Amy returns to Telegraph Creek to maintain her roots, tag along with Dad on his annual hunt and confidently share her new perspective on the world: "You think you can sit around and let the Indian woman do everything? We're liberated now." Still, the word "deli" filled me with hope of whole-grain bagels and pastrami on rye around the campfire. As fate would have it, though, I would be condemned to a diet little better than that endured by the poorest, mangiest Klondiker. Amy would seldom rise above Kraft Dinner, canned beans, and raspberry-flavoured Wagon Wheels.

Our gang also includes Fletcher's grandson Shane Quock, a pretentious smart aleck but also a fearless horseman who delights in galloping at breakneck speed. When he learns I am coming along on the trail ride, he looks at me disparagingly and asks, "How many times have you ridden?" Like a horse trader checking teeth, he inspects my muscles and concludes, "You'll do." Then, before turning away, he checks out his own reflection in my sunglasses. "Oh, looks good."

Rounding out the contingent is Ben Dubeau, a horse-logger from Hazelton in the Bulkley Valley of west-central British Columbia. A former teenage jockey, Dubeau is a tireless worker, skilled at packing horses and cunning at the hunt. He can easily spot distant game no bigger than a flea on an elephant's butt. We dub him the Marlboro Man for the way he slouches around the campfire, cigarette drooping from under his cowboy hat. A thoughtful man with a dry sense of humour, he delights in story telling. "I used to rodeo every summer on the northern circuit. My nickname was Ben Who? One year I figure I set an altitude record in every arena in B.C." Dubeau can employ all the diplomatic qualities necessary to handle the diverse nationalities that share his campfire. "Get a bunch of Germans together and they feel peer pressure," he explains. "Americans are easier going. Mexicans are a lot of fun, but you have to hold them back."

As for myself, what are my qualifications for a six-day wilderness horse ride? In Grade 12, I entered a bareback bronc rodeo competition at Williams Lake without the slightest idea of how to ride a horse but thinking, hell, it's only eight seconds. The last thing I remember before hitting the sawdust arena face first was the wooden chute opening and a fellow poking an electric prod into my horse, and taunting, "Go, Sawbuck." I didn't care much for riding horses after that. Not until four years ago, when, on assignment for *Canadian Geographic* magazine, I spent six days on horseback patrol with a provincial conservation officer in the Cassiar Mountains near Dease Lake. It was a good experience, and I carry one important lesson from that adventure—never be fooled into thinking your horse likes you.

My gelding steed for this trip is Casper, and he has every reason not to like me; Casper is twenty-one and I am asking him to carry me for six days across some of the most rugged terrain in this province. Am I expecting too much? I mean, why don't I just walk

Pack trains were indispensable at the turn of the century, hauling supplies during both the Klondike gold rush and completion of the Yukon telegraph line. Today, pack horses remain invaluable to guide-outfitters on wilderness hunts. (B.C. Archives and Records Service)

into an old folks' home, jump on the back of the first senior citizen I meet, and shout "Giddyap!" Fletcher assures me Casper is capable of the task, a gentle, reliable steed with but one idiosyncrasy—a fear of mud. Well, isn't that just great? According to all the Klondike diaries I've read, the Teslin Trail is a euphemism for mud —an endless sea of sticky, sopping mud that sucked the will out of the most determined prospector and left his horses exhausted and malnourished. Into this landscape I am riding a horse that fears mud.

At least I have the benefit of a hundred years of hindsight. The original Klondikers were led blindly into this unknown territory by false government promises, by merchants interested only in a fast buck, and by newspapers that relied on pure hearsay for their stories. Vancouver's *Province* newspaper had described the Teslin Trail as "passing through an exceptionally easy country," while the Victoria *Daily Colonist*, in supporting the Stikine route to the Klondike, referred to the trail as "but a short portage before the chain of waters leading to the upper Yukon." Having successfully traversed the route, Private Edward Lester concluded that "either the people who wrote about the trail were grossly ignorant regarding its conditions or they were affected with a complaint of which the most characteristic symptom is an unparalleled love of exaggeration and misrepresentation."

But misinformation about the Teslin Trail extended well beyond the popular press. In its January 1898 edition, the trade publication *British Columbia Mining Record* questioned the extent of the Klondike goldfields and warned that 80 percent of those making their way to Dawson "have never handled a pick or shovel, never packed fifty pounds on their back, put 200 pounds on a Cayuse,

Although pack animals served a vital role in the opening of the Canadian North, countless mules, horses and even dogs were worked to death during the Klondike gold rush. (B.C. Archives and Records Service)

cooked the lovely but indigestible flapjack and to whom as yet beans and bacon is an unknown luxury." The mining journal further predicted that only half the goldseekers would make it to Dawson, and many of those who did would never actually mine for gold. This was insightful commentary for its day, even if territorial jealousy between British Columbia and the Yukon might have played a part. Yet on the subject of the Teslin Trail, the *Mining Record* was as ignorant as everyone else. It compounded its mistake by running a first-person account of travelling up the frozen

Stikine River the previous January. "Travel by night was as brisk as day," according to the story. "We could see every night hundreds of lanterns glimmering like will-o'-the-wisps up and down the river in the dark." Although the correspondent turned around at Telegraph Creek and returned to Wrangell, he could not resist providing an ill-formed opinion of the Teslin Trail. "The country from Telegraph Creek to Teslin is flat and easily travelled, and pack trains can be hired at the former place at relatively reasonable rates." The *Mining Record*'s ultimate advice was: "Beyond this point a good trail will be open next year...indeed, a fair trail exists there even now."

Miners arrived in Glenora and Telegraph Creek in 1898 to find only disappointment and despair. Pack animals were scarce because the Yukon Field Force had priority. Freight services were exorbitant. The price of provisions had doubled or tripled since they left Victoria—bacon now selling at sixteen cents a pound, sugar at eleven cents, dried apricots at fifteen cents, beans at six cents. And the Teslin Trail, the only route north to Teslin Lake, some 250 kilometres away, was not a wagon road at all but a narrow, rutted, bug-ridden, swampy path to hell.

Despite the odds, some miners persisted northward, paring down their provisions, pushing wheelbarrows, scrounging food and blankets from fellow travellers, making do with the most pitiful-looking pack animals ever to serve a gold rush—horses, mules, oxen, even goats. And when they became mired in the mud and could proceed no farther, they were summarily executed with a shot to the head and left to rot or fed to the dogs. Some, like rancher Norman Lee from British Columbia's central Chilcotin region, even herded cattle or sheep over the Teslin Trail for sale to the hungry miners of Dawson. Lee's diary hints at the chaos: "With difficulty, I scared up a packtrain of nine half-dead animals—sores all over them, and so forth, about $20 a head—the price somehow goes up when one wants to buy."

By comparison, Casper doesn't seem so bad. He is old, but with age comes wisdom, and I conclude there is much he can teach me about life on the trail. Before bed on our first night, the horses are shuffled across a bridge to the other side of the river where there is better pasture. It is cold, and I give one of my wool sweaters to Shane as insurance. Just before crawling into my sleeping bag, I watch a gentle swath of northern lights wander over the seamless spruce forest. Then, as I am about to fall asleep, the long wavering howl of a wolf pack rises like a cloud of steam from the woods. According to one native legend, the howls are the cries of lost souls seeking to return to earth. Perhaps that's why the sound stirs an inner restlessness in me. I sense that the trail ahead is paved with as much excitement, hardship and personal discovery as it was a century ago. Only the most cynical armchair adventurer would suggest that a Gore-Tex jacket or propane camp stove takes the romance out of a wilderness challenge in the Canadian North.

The next day we rise at 8 a.m., but the business of eating and packing up takes six hours. As we prepare to move out in brilliant sunshine—five riders, eight packhorses, and three spares—Casper rebels before I am even in the saddle. He is spooked by a piece of tissue paper drifting across the ground and steps on my toe. This is not the way to begin a beautiful relationship. Following an old Indian trail, Fletcher takes the lead, I ride a close second and the others space out along the pack train. When we encounter fallen trees across our path, Fletcher either leads us around them or dismounts from his buckskin horse and reaches for a single-bladed axe from the left side of his saddle. A few well-chosen blows and the trail is clear again. "I heard the camp robber talking to me when I was cutting the trail, so I knew it would be okay," he says of the ubiquitous grey jay, better known as the whisky jack. The route through pine, poplar and spruce offers pleasant views of the river below us, but one cannot become careless. Brush is forever whacking you in the face, an errant limb aiming to dislodge a hat or an eyeball. Horses are equally vulnerable. "These dry broken sticks are dangerous," he shouts back. "They'll go right through a horse's gut."

Fletcher points out a spot on the trail where a wolf has been scratching around in the dirt. He will shoot dead any wolf he sees on the trail, and he keeps a .375 Winchester rifle by his side, just in case. Like most guide-outfitters, he views wolves as a direct threat to his livelihood, taking out game that a foreign hunter might pay US$10,000 or more for the privilege of shooting. It is nothing personal, he assures me—just business. But I cannot help thinking that if the wolf cannot exist free in this remote wilderness because it competes with rich foreigners, then game management has advanced little beyond the days of the bounty. I suspect it will not change much, either, until provincial authorities see all wildlife as having an intrinsic equal value. But Fletcher says there is no reason to worry about the wolf—not for the time being, not around this wilderness region. "They'll never clean the wolf out. They're like dogs. They'll always be around."

The author, posing with a rifle in front of an old telegraph line cabin on the Little Tahltan River, attempts to relive a scene from the past on the Stikine route to the Klondike. (Shane Quock)

By 6 p.m. we are approaching a salmon enhancement camp on the Little Tahltan River, an important spawning stream. Staff here operate a gate across the river, marking fish and keeping count: a total of 6,800 chinook to date. "A Dutch man and his son hiked this way, headed for Atlin, last year," recalls Colin Barnard, the contractor in charge, a bear of a man sitting in a big wooden chair christened "General Patton." "We heard someone shout, 'Hey,' and almost jumped out of our skin. Hammers and nails all over the place. They were both in the Dutch special forces. They made it all the way through." That is only mildly encouraging news. The Yukon telegraph line paralleled the Teslin Trail north from Telegraph Creek only to a point near the Nahlin River, a distance of about 150 kilometres. Then the telegraph line forked to the northwest, toward the community of Atlin, while the Teslin Trail continued north toward Teslin Lake. The route of the telegraph line should be in better shape than the route to Teslin Lake; after all, the line continued to operate for years after the Klondike gold rush. There is no reason to believe that the upper portions of the Teslin Trail will be equally passable. No reason at all.

In the early evening we approach Saloon, a point on the river named after a small settlement occupied during the Klondike rush, where we connect with the Teslin Trail. "There was a guy who had a keg of rum and sold it by the drink to people going by," says Fletcher. "That's where the name comes from." A small, moth-eaten cabin comes into view, but Fletcher dismisses it as a relic of the telegraph line, not the Klondike rush. "There used to be quite a few cabins up on the bench," he reflects. "An older brother of mine drowned here, right near the Indian camp. He was just three or four years old. They figured he was throwing rocks at seagulls and slipped. I was just a baby." Just up ahead on the trail, Fletcher signals my attention as a grizzly sow and two cubs catch wind of us and scamper into the bushes. Their handiwork is everywhere around us. Rotting salmon corpses hauled up onto the shore—brains and skin gutted for their high nutrition, much of the remainder left to rot. As we enter this scene of biological devastation, Fletcher quietly announces, "Let's make camp." Sure, why not? Maybe we could sleep with a ring of garlic sausage around our necks, too, tonight, just in case the bears don't get the message.

During a lull in the camp activity before dusk, Shane and I sneak out for a walk to the telegraph-line cabin we passed earlier. Walking with a rifle for protection, we watch for bulky silhouettes amid the infernal splashing of spawning fish. After a few quick photographs, each of us posing with the rifle outside the door, we head back to the security of the campfire.

The nightly campfire stories are already well under way. "A half-breed is the ruination of the Indian tribe and an improvement to white men," laughs Fletcher, washing that one down with a shot of rum. "You know, the nice thing about being half Indian and half white is that you can play cowboys and Indians by yourself." In a stuffy urban atmosphere, remarks like those could put some people into a counselling program for weeks. In their fight for a socially sterile world, they cannot relate to the reality of life, especially that of rural areas not yet poisoned by political correctness. Nor can they appreciate that the first step to personal enlightenment is as simple as not taking yourself too seriously.

I am starting to hate early mornings and the tedious job of

*Guide outfitter and Tahltan Indian Fletcher Day admires the view
from Kennicott Lake while traversing the historic Teslin Trail,
part of the all-Canadian route to the Klondike gold rush.*
(Larry Pynn)

packing up, balancing the grub boxes, cinching them up tightly on
each packhorse. These plastic boxes take a beating, being forever
scraped or beaten by the passing brush. It takes hours to set them
up correctly, and I cannot develop the knack for it. All those years
of experience don't make it any easier for Fletcher, either. "I don't
know how many times I've been looking forward to that last horse.

The Yukon telegraph line and the Teslin Trail followed the same
route through much of the Stikine Plateau north of Telegraph
Creek. This photo, taken in 1956 near the old Hyland ranch,
shows the route was still clear nearly half a century ago.
(B.C. Archives and Records Service)

When I was nineteen years old, I broke camp 72 times in 120 days."
As much as we hate it, we know we have to do it right the first
time or face the distasteful prospect of a second attempt down the
trail under conditions almost certainly more difficult.

On our second day, the spruce deadfall gets worse on the trail,
forcing Fletcher to dismount repeatedly, muttering epithets all the
way. Just a year ago he cleared much of this trail with an axe and
a chainsaw. But a heavy snow last fall broke off many branches
before the trees had a chance to freeze solid. Fletcher refuses to
relinquish the clearing job to anyone else, figuring there's only one
way to keep his axe sharp. By 1:30 p.m., we leave the Little Tahltan
River and proceed from the Stikine River drainage to the Taku
River watershed. The terrain ranges from areas of rock slides to
swampy marsh, and our route is shrouded by tall cranberry and
Saskatoon berry bushes. Some sections are unforgivingly steep.
"Don't pull back or you'll go right over," Fletcher cautions, leaning
heavily forward in the saddle. Downhill slopes are no easier, the
horses sliding their way over the trail, my head pressed flat against
Casper's butt.

Breaking free from the bush at a quiet lake, we stop to watch
a cow moose and calf on the far shore. Fletcher complains that the
modern topo maps call this place Kennicott Lake, after a mining
company, but he refuses to recognize it. *New York* was the name of
a boat that ferried Klondikers across the lake during the gold rush,
so New York Lake it is. Navigating a narrow wisp of trail at the
end of the lake, he reflects, "This trail used to be four feet wide.
We used to lead teams of horses through here and now there's just
room for a single."

Near 4 p.m. we pass Dead Horse Camp, the place where a horse died a year ago after becoming entangled in its hobbles. All that remains today are a couple of bones here, a hoof there. Such tragic accidents are relatively rare these days. The creed of today's back-country horseman is "Care for your steed first, yourself second, because the horse is going to get you both home." The pack animal that walked this trail a century ago enjoyed no such respect. Some of the worst atrocities man has ever inflicted on the domestic animal occurred during the Klondike gold rush. Skinny, sore-infested packhorses, mules, and oxen fell by the wayside like wartime casualties, crippled by mistreatment, gruelling conditions, and lack of forage. When one finally, mercifully, slumped over dead, its load was transferred to the remaining pack animals until they, too, gave up the ghost, and the miner had no alternative but to throw away or sell at bargain-basement prices everything he could not carry on his own back: saddles, shovels, picks.

Fletcher knows the stories only too well. His stepfather, Ira Day, was a gold-hungry, Nebraskan twenty-one-year-old when he arrived at the Stikine River in the fall of 1898. He would later confirm the horrible overland conditions and how his exhausted pack burros, mired in the mud and unable to walk farther, were left behind to die. "Even as an old man, he said he could remember the sound of those burros," Fletcher recalls with a wince. "He didn't have the heart to shoot them."

Eventually, we pass pioneer Bob Hyland's old ranch, now owned by another guide-outfitter and marked by a flat, open meadow, remnants of a corral, and a few old log buildings. One of the cabins is in liveable condition—or was. A grizzly has crawled inside and ransacked the place. Plastic windows torn out. Pots, pans, and chopped wood all over. Salt and pepper strewn around. A giant tooth hole in an old tin of strawberry jam. Not a huge mess, but not the kind of scene one wants to encounter after a long trail ride. Besides, the bear that develops a knack for breaking and entering is a menace. Success can be as sweet as honey, fiendishly drawing the bruin from one cabin to the next.

After a brief lunch, we press on toward the Sheslay River, site of one of Fletcher's base camps and a former Tahltan Indian settlement. By 8:30 p.m., after a luxuriously cool evening ride, the camp comes into view. We pass an old cabin with a white cross, evidence that Catholic priests used to visit the Tahltans at the winter traplines by the Sheslay River. Ah, signs of civilization are just around the corner—airstrip, generator, cook house, running water, individual cabins. And none too soon. It's been a long day, and everyone can feel it. Seconds later, however, our dream of an oasis turns into an ugly nightmare. The main lodge has been raided. And this time the bear left nothing untouched. Fletcher is furious. He lent the place to a couple of American fishing friends a few weeks earlier, and they carelessly left food on the counter, an invitation to the first bear to break in and investigate. We are all dejected. Rather than finding a refuge from the day's ride, the camp represents a day's delay while we have to work long and hard getting it back into some semblance of order. For Fletcher, this place houses too many bad memories. It was here, two years ago, that his wife shot him four times with a .22 handgun. Added to the irony, she is already back in Telegraph Creek after serving eight months of her sentence. It gets worse. As part of the couple's divorce settlement, they are splitting the guiding territory, and this particular hunting base camp goes to her. Fletcher doesn't say so, but you can just hear him thinking: "She's gonna kill me. This time, she's really gonna kill me."

We walk into the cabin on egg shells. Exactly how bad is it? Real bad. No gang of vandals could come close to this bear's accomplishment. "That pisses me off," says Fletcher, holding up a door pulled right off the propane cook stove. "I just bought that stove new." All the food in the kitchen is strewn around or shredded—cocoa and coffee, onions and potatoes, curry. The foam mattress in the side bedroom is ripped apart. And every window is destroyed, supporting Fletcher's belief that bears never leave a cabin through the window by which they enter. "Watch for that son of a bitch," he growls. "If he pokes his nose out, I'll shoot him." But the bear does not show. Having consumed a twenty-two-kilogram sack of sugar, the bastard quite possibly blew himself to pieces. We figure justice prevailed.

Eventually, the shock of the mess passes and the inevitability of our task takes hold. We get the generator going for light and push the worst of the debris aside so we can eat dinner. With another well-deserved shot of rum, Fletcher eventually adopts a stoical attitude that is typical of native people. "There was too much junk in here anyway. It's time to clean it out." Having a bear rip through your place can turn your perspective upside down, too. When I spot a mouse navigating the kitchen's copper plumbing, Fletcher remarks, "You know, we used to be worried if a mouse got in here. This place was supposed to be mouseproof."

With a broom in hand, Amy looks outside at the last beams of light breaking on Kaketsa Mountain in the distance, a scene that stirs a flood of warm childhood memories. As an eleven-year-old she spent a winter here on the trapline—seven children and two parents in two tents with temperatures as cold as minus 45 degrees Fahrenheit. "Those were my fondest memories that winter," she confides. "I never went to school, but I got a different kind of schooling."

Toward the end of the next day, the floors are mopped, the garbage taken out and the windows repaired. It is time for an eerie sidetrip, to Sheslay Mike's place, barely a kilometre away. Shane fires up the motorized all-terrain vehicle, and we drive down the airstrip to a riverside log cabin. Not just any log cabin, mind you. Built as an octagon—hand-peeled logs chinked with moss, the roof an intricate tapestry of interlocking pieces—the cabin is among the most elaborate you could find in the Canadian North. Too elaborate, perhaps. Such attention to detail gives evidence not only of a skilled craftsman but, under these conditions, of a strange mind, the crazed rationale of Michael Eugene Oros, a man who roamed the British Columbia-Yukon border like a rabid animal, instilling fear wherever he went. A loner who grew up in small-town Kansas, Oros settled in the Stikine country during the 1970s, living off the land and learning what he could from the Indians. But with each passing day he became wilder than the land, stealing from cabins and talking about a conspiracy by the CIA, FBI and RCMP to spray him with chemicals and make him insane.

In 1981, an Atlin trapper named Gunter Hans Lishy went missing while illegally working a native trapline at Hutsigola Lake. Police investigating Lishy's disappearance found some of his

Logs cut from standing timber created a road that helped horses haul supplies during completion of the Yukon telegraph line in the years following the Klondike gold rush. (B.C. Archives and Records Service)

personal effects at Oros's cabin in 1982 but lacked sufficient evidence to lay any charges more serious than possession of stolen property. That really unnerved northern residents. The thought of a crazed killer roaming the wilderness with impunity was enough to keep people out of the bush altogether. Then, in March 1985, another trapper reported a theft from his cabin on the west side of Teslin Lake, about eighty kilometres south of the community of Teslin. The trapper fingered Oros as the culprit. Finally—something solid to go on. When Oros fired at an aircraft flown in to check him out, there was no turning back. It was time to take down the mad dog. But Oros wasn't going easily, not with his uncanny bush sense and unbridled sense of paranoia. The next day an RCMP emergency response team assembled in the bush alongside Teslin Lake, waiting for Oros to make his way toward them and for the inevitable gun battle to unfold. It proved to be a poorly executed plan that seriously underestimated their suspect's skill and determination. Oros crept up from behind and drew first blood, killing young Constable Michael Buday with a single shot to the ear from a .303 bolt-action rifle. Then he reloaded, took aim at Buday's partner, Constable Garry Rodgers, and fired again. In that instant a sonic boom of rifle fire shattered the clear winter air. Another man dropped to the snow with a fatal bullet wound in his head. It was Oros. His gun had misfired, and Rodgers seized the moment to get off one quick round, an incredibly accurate shot that seemed to fly through the forest with spiritual intervention. The bloody affair was over, and yet another mad-trapper legend had begun.

Oros hated Fletcher. He talked of killing him, of getting even for Fletcher's complaining to the authorities about him. That didn't surprise Fletcher. "He came here as a young fellow, only eighteen years old," he recalls. "As he got older, he got worse. He was trapping beaver out of season on my trapline. I turned him in, and the game wardens came and took all his stuff away from him. I never did see him again. But he was after me. He knew I was the one who turned him in. I didn't take anything too seriously." But the threats had a real basis. After Oros was shot dead, the ensuing investigation turned up a skull and scattered bones near his cabin. They were Lishy's remains. Eventually, a coroner's jury in 1986 would close the case, determining that Lishy had died of a gunshot. Oros had shot him in the back.

The next day we are back on the trail by noon, a ninety-minute uphill trip to Sheslay Summit, a sub-alpine zone that is also the highest point on the Teslin Trail. "Look at that," Fletcher remarks. "No soapberries. No wonder the bears are so hungry." For no particular reason, except perhaps that the longer you are in the bush the more the mind thinks of the finer things in life, Fletcher remarks that he is getting married next winter to a nurse in Smithers. A Caribbean honeymoon cruise with a country music theme is planned: steel guitars and steel drums. No, I can't see it, either. But what the hell, Fletcher can. "I've tried marriage to two Indian women," he muses. "Now I'm going to try a white one."

At a telegraph-line cabin, we stop for a bite to eat and poke around. In a corner of the cabin lies an old mattress and a few pots and pans believed left behind by Sheslay Mike. Fletcher points to the asphalt roof as the reason telegraph-line cabins are still standing while those built with dirt roofs have collapsed. Inside, on a log over the door frame, Fletcher's name is scrawled and dated October 1955 (exactly eight months after I was born), when he was packing for a prospecting trip. "The longest I spent in school was thirty days," he reflects. "Just long enough to learn to sign my name."

Later, on the trail, we discover a huge pine stump, a former mile-post on the Teslin Trail that marked fifty miles to Telegraph Creek and fifty miles to the Nahlin River. Then we cross Race Flats, a sprawling amber meadow, flush with new grass for the horses. "The horses would eat themselves so fat they couldn't move if it wasn't for the mosquitoes," Fletcher informs us. "It's all in God's plan." Alongside the trail, stretches of telegraph wire hang like clothes-line, waiting to ensnare the first moose or caribou that passes this way. I know just how dangerous it can be. A year earlier, during my hike through the Mackenzie Mountains following the Canol oil pipeline, I saw the antlers of a bull caribou that had died after becoming ensnared with wire so tough you needed pliers to bend it. I'd hate to guess how many other animals die needlessly every year because of man's refusal to clean up a little garbage. Almost simultaneously, Fletcher's horse baulks as its feet catch in a stretch of the century-old snare. "A lot of grouse were cut in half by the line," says Fletcher, ever so gently working his horse free from the mess. "It's very strong." The horses don't need any more grief. Flu is spreading among them, leaving them tired and listless. One horse has an eye closed shut, and pus oozes up in the eyes of the others. "It won't hurt them any," Fletcher assures me. "I just brought a new horse up here and they all got it from him."

The Teslin Trail ahead of us is nothing more than a foot-deep trench engulfed on both sides by head-high willows and dwarf birch. Unfolding in the distance are the rolling Stikine Plateau and Heart Peaks—prime caribou and mountain sheep habitat, so named, says Fletcher, because the range resembles a moose heart on a platter. In wetter sections of the trail the horses are occasionally buoyed up by remnants of the old corduroy road laid during the Klondike rush. The spruce logs, laid crosswise like railway ties, are in amazingly good condition, artifacts preserved over time by the northern deep-freeze winters. Then, just before we reach Ball Lake around 7 p.m., the inevitable happens. Mud!!! Old Casper is up to his belly in it, wired with panic, heaving back and forth like a locomotive. He lunges forward and lands heavily on his chest, the mud pulling him down like a thousand hands dripping with glue and malice. That's it: I'm outta here. With a strong frog-like push from the stirrups, I leap clear of the horse to the side, landing heavily in the mud. A quick shedding of seventy kilograms is just what Casper needed. With one or two more powerful lunges, he is back on his feet and walking shakily to drier ground. It could have been worse, Fletcher comments. Once he poked a three-metre-long stick into a mud hole and still didn't hit bottom. Then Shane rides up and offers, "It's official. You're a rodeo rider."

After spending the night at Wolf Camp, an open stand of pine trees near Cache Creek, we find the trail dry and easy going. Or so we think. Goldie, one of the packhorses on only her second trip, suddenly becomes spooked when a branch snaps. She goes crazy. And I mean crazzzzzzy. With reckless abandon, she tears through the forest, oblivious to the trail, ploughing through branches and kicking up her heels in sheer insanity. We all do our best to hold position and not spark a stampede, tying the horses to trees with their halters. After several long minutes, Goldie, out of steam and pack boxes dislodged, is rounded up and returned to her place in the pack train. In time, Fletcher assures me, she will become accustomed to her wilderness lot, will become so hardened she will not even eat an apple offered her. "These are good packhorses. They don't know any other life."

In mid-afternoon, Fletcher makes a wrong turn in a sea of tall willows, an expanse so large that only the tops of the riders' heads are visible as they float along from white cap to white cap. It turns out to be a short diversion; an hour later, we are back on the trail again, passing Lost Lake and the old Callison Ranch site en route to our final camp together on the Koshin River. But this simple, brief mistake by the man with the greatest current knowledge of the Teslin Trail highlights the impenetrable nature of this land a century after the human flood to the Klondike. Nature can indeed be an efficient undertaker. If anything, the Teslin Trail goes through wilder country today. All that remains is a narrow, rutted horse path, a few lengths of telegraph wire, bits of corduroy logs and a handful of decaying log cabins. Few routes in North America can claim to have receded so effectively from the tides of civilization. And now it is this wilderness vacuum into which I must walk alone.

With portions of the Teslin Trail overgrown with willows, guide-outfitter Fletcher Day is one of the few people who still uses the historic route to access summer hunting grounds. (Larry Pynn)

7

NO MAN'S LAND

Where Fletcher Day travels is no-man's-land, but there are places where even he does not go. And I am going to one such place. Fletcher does not share my enthusiasm for continuing north on the Teslin Trail. Ahead lie merciless swarms of mosquitoes and an ungodly world of swamps and bogs. He has been there before, and he has no desire to return. To emphasize the point, shortly before we part he hands me a rabbit's foot—not the soft, buffed type but the gnawed and scruffy real McCoy—and says prophetically, "There is nothing up there. Just keep to the trail." It is difficult not to respect Fletcher, who, after all, has survived four gunshot wounds and can still drink water without leaking all over the place. But this time I hope he is wrong. With a final handshake, I wade across the Koshin River, accompanied only by Shane on horseback. He follows me to the river's edge, then hands me a pack of chewing gum and a small compliment. "It's gonna feel strange without you," he confesses. "Don't get lost, Larry."

As I melt into the forest, my emotions fluctuate between excitement and trepidation. The sky is robin's-egg blue, and the air is sweet and warm. But an ill wind is blowing my way. Compared with the relatively spit-and-polish portion of the Teslin Trail traversed so far with Fletcher, this section has all but yielded to the elements. Faint and littered with deadfall, the trail forces me to make repeated detours through thick brush. I lose the route entirely through swamps, only picking it up by a series of methodical sweeps. "It was a pretty awful hike," I record grimly in my diary. "Ploughing through head-high willows and around deadfall, and lots of marsh. I'm a little apprehensive about the rest of my trip if its gets any worse."

At times like this, even the smallest evidence of the gold rush seems like the mother lode—a pole teetering in the distance, a tangled stretch of telegraph line, the skeletal remains of a cabin or a rotting remnant of corduroy road. I even claim a heavy white porcelain insulator as a souvenir, but liberating it is no easy chore. Prying away the stiff, galvanized telegraph wire is like removing a hand in rigor mortis, one finger at a time.

I proceed with the reverence of a walk in a cemetery. This forest is habitat for far too many ghosts. The spirits of the Klondikers seemingly dance among the shafts of sunlight piercing the canopy. My pack is heavy, to be sure, but it is no match for the weight hauled by some of those prospectors of a century ago. They carried so many provisions and mining supplies they were forced to shuttle them back and forth, a tedious, heart-wrenching task. "We started the long trek to Teslin with five loads for a hand sled," recalled Darius Barry, a Newfoundlander who captained a halibut boat in the North Pacific before tackling the Klondike in the winter of 1897-98. "That meant we'd take one load for a certain distance,

A typical log cabin used by linemen performing maintenance on the Yukon telegraph line, completed between Dawson and Vancouver shortly after the Klondike gold rush. (B.C. Archives and Records Service)

then go back for another, repeating the process until all five loads were moved forward as far as possible every day. It was tough going, 45-50 degrees below all winter. We had a tent and at night we'd put it up and make a bed of evergreen boughs. Then have a supper of frozen beans. Then we'd get up in the morning and push on in that roadless wilderness, breaking trail on snowshoes." Barry made it to Dawson City in July 1898 at the peak of the gold rush and staked his claim. He never got rich, but he stayed healthy—had not so much as a cold—and returned home to Victoria with a few nuggets as souvenirs in 1900.

Shortly before dusk of the first day alone, I reach the Nahlin River, a former station site on the old Vancouver-to-Dawson telegraph line. Telegraph cabins were usually maintained by two men, an operator to relay and receive messages, a lineman to keep the wire in good shape, and were supplied by horse pack trains. Guy Lawrence served with the telegraph service from 1902 until 1946, when much of the line had already become obsolete. Some of his most memorable days were spent at the Nahlin River, socializing with the Tahltans, trapping in winter to supplement his income, and traipsing around the countryside in all kinds of weather to solve all manner of problems. This far from civilization, he was called upon to perform tasks that went well beyond his official job description. On one occasion in 1905, he carried out the marriage rites for a young Tahltan man who, against his elders' wishes, had chosen a bride from outside the tribe. "Bidding the two to stand up and hold hands, I read them a recipe from the small cook book my mother had sent me." There is still a trapper's cabin here, but the main living quarters are locked up, a reflection of changing attitudes even in the remote North, where cabins were once open to anyone who needed them. This trapper has at least settled for a compromise, leaving open a cubbyhole of a room with a wood-stove in case of emergency. In the cold grip of winter this place might look inviting. But not tonight. I proceed straight to the river, thankful to find a cable crossing over the swift-flowing, waist-high water. I pull myself across, one hand over the other, while sitting on a small platform. Then I establish base camp over a happy-hour combo of coffee and chocolate.

Minutes later, while cooking up my spiciest dehydrated dinner, I watch a lynx emerge from the alder bush downwind and across the river. The cat sits patiently in the shoreline shadows, its nose twitching furiously to decipher my culinary Morse code. But when I move carefully to the tent to fetch my camera, the lynx vanishes, another ghost of the forest. That night I fall asleep to the sound of scratching from a spruce tree twenty metres away on the riverbank. I assume it's the work of a porcupine, but it could just as easily be a grizzly. Quite frankly, I am too tired to care.

Soon after I start out the next morning, the trail divides, the left fork, the Telegraph Trail, leading to the tiny British Columbia mining town of Atlin, the right fork, the Teslin Trail, heading due north to Teslin Lake. At first I find the Teslin route in surprisingly good shape, kept cleared by a local trapper, and by noon Gun Lake emerges on my right. While at the Sheslay River camp, Fletcher Day reported hearing radio-phone traffic from the trapper's cabin just up the side of the lake. In case of trouble, he suggested, make my way to that cabin. I shout, but there is no answer. The cabin is not in sight, and I have far to travel. I push onward through increasingly difficult terrain until the trail peters out. No amount of searching or backtracking can bring it back this time. Starting a small smudge fire to fend off mosquitoes so tenacious they threaten to carry me away, I consult the topographical map I am using to guide me. The map has a clear dotted line marking a route almost as old as Canada that once led other men as foolish and adventurous as I through this section of the Teslin Trail. Unequivocal as it is about this trail of '98, the map lies. The dotted line is now history, so to speak, no more than a series of moose paths leading inevitably to frustration and disappointment.

I cannot say I am entirely surprised. Research has told me I am neither the first journalist to venture this way nor the first person to be appalled by the difficult conditions. Correspondent Faith Fenton traversed this section in a long dress and mosquito-net headgear in 1898 with her Yukon Field Force escort. Her description sounds bleak: "...we see on either side of us as far as our vision extends nothing but low lying bog.... Sometimes it is dry and towy, oftener it is wet and spongy, centering in a perfect slough...in which the poor pack mule sinks and is helpless." Edward Lester, the Field Force private, recorded an even more depressing passage: "We are either tramping through the bog moss, beaten by the feet of many pack mules into black unfathomable depths, or with equal difficulty scrambling, crawling, making our way over miles upon miles of ground blackened by prostrate logs."

In a report on his exploration in 1897 for a railway and wagon route between Telegraph Creek and Teslin Lake, federal civil engineer William Tyndale Jennings described the northern terrain as "covered with moss and occasionally mire and unpleasant to travel over in unseasonal weather." To overcome such conditions, he recommended removing the top layer of lumpy moss and cutting a ten-foot swath through the boreal forest to let in the sunlight and allow the soil to dry. Soft, mushy ground should be covered with brush, he said, and "top-dressed" with coarse gravel or broken stone and ditched to allow runoff of water. He estimated that such a project would take two months to complete at a cost of $100 to

$2.50 per mile. Because of the lack of natural forage along the route and the anticipated heavy traffic, the government should also provide a number of cache houses for the use of packers and the storage of feed. "A trail so constructed would ensure good footing on ground so compact as not to be churned into holes, ruts and mire in wet weather," he concluded. We shall never know whether Jennings's recommendations, had they not been ignored by the federal government, would actually have worked. The presence of permafrost—permanently frozen ground, found on a hit-or-miss basis in northern British Columbia—might in fact have worsened trail conditions. Even half a century later, during construction of the Alaska Highway in 1942, the United States army was discovering the hard way that the only way to deal with permafrost is to build on top of it. Removal of the surface layer only allows the frozen ground to thaw out, rendering it a swamp of impenetrable muck.

In his diary, Private Lester makes reference to the infernal smoke from forest fires, the result of miners' carelessly abandoning their campfires and allowing the flames to smoulder in the soft, hummocky moss. He wrote: "These hundreds of square miles of excellent timber must have been destroyed through the selfish indifference of men who would not stretch out a hand for a pail of water to save from destruction millions of cords of wood which did not belong to them." Forest fires were so pervasive along the Teslin Trail that Arthur Saint Cyr, a surveyor exploring the country east of Teslin Lake for the Department of the Interior, was unable to take bearings from the nearby mountain tops because of all the smoke. Conditions were no better on the Yukon River. A traveller named Julius Price noted that "the whole country was ablaze from the banks of the river to the summits of the highest hills where there was timber to burn, and I feel much inclined to add that in my opinion if there is no heavy rain to check these fires, there will scarcely be a particle of timber left growing in the country in a year's time." I can only assume that at least some of the blackened rotting logs I see strewn around the landscape are remnants of those fires.

I have little choice but to ignore the dotted line on my map and make my way purely by map and compass. It is a hellish job. Open stretches of marsh are inevitably followed by spruce forest so thick it blots out the sun and obliterates all landmarks. A life-giving lake could be forty metres to my left or to my right and I would be none the wiser. Did I say a lake? I wish. By mid-afternoon I find a turbid pond and slog my way to the water's edge, siphoning out water for boiling within a stick's throw of a beaver lodge. An osprey circles slowly overhead, but it might as well be a vulture. Boiled for ten minutes and spiked with orange crystals to make it mildly appealing, this foul liquid is my only comfort in this hellish wasteland.

Nightfall finds me deep in the forest, too tired to make dinner, low on water and surrounded by mosquitoes. Setting out alone, I had hoped to learn more about those haggard old gold miners of yore—and about myself. Now, two days into my solo hike, I find that the lessons are coming fast and hard. My diary reflects the depth of my despair and just how close I have come to sharing the hopelessness of those despondent Klondikers of a century ago. "This has been one of the longest days of my life," I write in my diary. "It just went on and on and on. The spruce forest is like walking on tires, up and down, no solid footing. Then marsh after marsh after marsh. It is horrible. Things are pretty hopeless at this point."

The next morning, I proceed for another hour or two until I can take no more—the heat, the thirst, the terrain, the sense of utter despair. When you're alone in the swamps of northern British Columbia, no one can hear you scream. And scream I do, wilting under an unrelenting sun, staggering under the weight of my backpack, tripping on the lumpy terrain and falling heavily face first into the mud and willows. At times like this, I feel justified in uttering the most vile epithets. But the wilderness landscape is in no mood to listen; it snuffs out my voice like a big suffocating pillow, yielding nothing, not even the echo of my own voice. With my shoulders turning blue from the constant chafing and my sore right knee beginning to buckle, I slam my pack to the ground.

I am a defeated man. I am turning back. To the north awaits Teslin Lake, barely seventy-five kilometres away but about as unattainable as the moon, with no trail through this alien landscape. Reluctantly, but confident that I am making the right decision, I decide to retrace my steps and make my stand at Gun Lake. There is really no choice. I lack the food for the lengthy hike back to Telegraph Creek, even if I could follow the overgrown trail accurately. No, Gun Lake it is. From there I will contemplate not only how I got into this predicament but also how to get out of it before I am reported missing to federal search-and-rescue officials.

If there is any consolation it is that I have a backup plan. I was to have rendezvoused with my friend Albrecht five days from now at the south end of Teslin Lake. If I miss the date, he is supposed to accompany the pilot of a chartered floatplane along my route until I am found. Then we will complete the all-Canadian route together, paddling down the Teslin and Yukon rivers to Dawson before the first flurries of snow. In the meantime, I will attempt to flag down the first aircraft that flies past. If I get into real trouble, my ace in the hole is an electronic locator transmitter (ELT), a device used on aircraft to send a satellite signal to search authorities in the event of a crash. The ELT is my insurance, but I am inclined to treat it more like dynamite. Once activated, it may well attract an expensive rescue mission that seems a highly inappropriate end to my solo hike.

Slogging one last time back through the bush, I reach Gun Lake the following day and find the trapper's tiny cabin, empty of life and secured with a padlock, on the west shore. Here, on a knoll of pines, I establish my camp, maintaining a fire all day every day in hopes of attracting an aircraft's attention. Meanwhile, I am not content to sit and wait. I commit my first break-and-enter, using a piece of angle iron found outside the cabin to pry out the metal screws holding the padlock. Hoping to find a mobile radiophone inside, I find only more disappointment and the usual trappings of a mountain man: steel Conibear killing traps, woodstove, foam mattress. Outside, however, I manage to scrounge enough old planks and aluminum sheets to create three large Xs on the hillside as an emergency signal to passing aircraft.

And they do fly past, but always tantalizingly out of range. One plane is too high to spot my magnesium-based emergency flare. Two others are within earshot, but out of sight of camp. All the while I am tormented by the flies, the wasps and, of course, the mosquitoes, which sound more like the drone of an aircraft with every passing day. "When you put them all together, they are a continual ongoing source of torment," I record in my diary. "They push

*Having arranged several aluminum sheets into a series of three
large Xs as an emergency signal, the stranded author watches
for passing aircraft on the shores of Gun Lake in northern
British Columbia.* (Larry Pynn)

your tolerance to the limit and beyond. I don't know, perhaps it is
like having kids, but with kids there are surely good days and bad
days. But with bugs, they are all bad all the time."

I cannot do anything very adventurous too far from camp, for fear of missing an aircraft. I busy myself trying to catch fish (without success), taking photos of myself bathing in the lake or peering into the distance with binoculars, and licking my wounds —swallowing doses of amoxicillin to ward off infection in the sores festering on my arms, legs and face. What's worse, I have developed a bad case of giardiasis, caused by a parasite that is passed on through animal feces, presumably from the water in the beaver pond. Until now, dinner time has been the one luxury I could look forward to. Now, even that pleasure has been taken from me; the moment food enters my mouth, my stomach tries its damnedest to squirt it out the other end.

As if infected by some insidious disease, my thoughts become irrational. I talk to the loons and myself. Fortunately, only the loons answer back. I see myself as a modern-day Robinson Crusoe, surviving for years in the wilderness before I am rescued and my story becomes the subject of a made-for-TV movie. I am even thinking twice about all those traps inside the cabin. If backed into a corner, I could live off squirrels, as many of the buck-toothed little buggers as it would take. Yes, survival on this knoll has become a matter of me versus them.

Beside the safe smudge of the campfire there is time to take stock of my supplies. My green army-surplus wool pants are in the worst shape, gaping holes patched together with strips of silver duct tape. On that score, I would not have looked out of place on the Teslin Trail a century ago. Harsh conditions caused even the best-planned expedition to travel short of supplies. When their horses gave out, the miners could carry only a fraction of what they needed. Cattleman Norman Lee walked sections of the trail with appallingly little, relying on the goodwill of fellow travellers to scrounge a meal of bacon and a blanket. "I was getting humble now—the night was cold," he wrote. "I asked the old man if he could spare me a saddle blanket or two to roll up in. He said, 'Stranger you are welcome to half what I have got.' Result, lots of bacon and blankets. That night one of the two burro died beside the old fellow's tent."

After five days, it is decision time. I am safe and secure here; I can remain indefinitely, waiting for the first aircraft to find my encampment. But I know I am past due for my rendezvous with Albrecht. Because he has not shown up with the chartered pilot, I take it for granted that someone has notified the authorities, and people are out searching for me. I persuade myself that if I activate the ELT, I will save everyone a lot of trouble by pinpointing my location. But I am wrong. Unknown to me, the chartered pilot has dropped Albrecht off at our rendezvous site at the south end of Teslin Lake. Rather than notify the RCMP that I am overdue in the wilderness and equipped with an ELT, he has decided to give me several more days to hike out before raising the alarm. When I do activate it, hoping to save searchers time, officials on the receiving end in Victoria can only assume the worst and initiate a full-fledged response to an air crash.

The next morning at about 8:30 a.m., I hear the unmistakable drone of a plane approaching from the west. It is a single-engined Cessna 172, high in the sky and conducting a series of transects in an effort to pinpoint my signal. I hurry to heap green boughs on the fire to create smoke and shoot off my second flare over the lake. Damn! The plane is actually flying away from me, but eventually it returns on a criss-cross pattern. Closer, closer.... Then, almost frantic, I fire off my third and last flare, feeling like a gunslinger expending his last round. Now I must watch and wait... and wait...until the plane suddenly changes direction and aims deliberately toward my position. Praise the Lord and the squirrels, I am found!

Circling low overhead several times to ensure I am all right, Summit Air pilot Jamie Tait from Atlin drops a note in a plastic bag weighted down with a wrench. It reads: "Your ELT has been found. We will send a floatplane out as soon as possible to pick you up." As he departs, I try to record my thoughts, but a lump in my throat stops me cold. Then I find the rabbit's foot Fletcher gave me and toss it into the campfire, concluding this is not the sort of luck I need. An hour later, elation fades to embarrassment. A helicopter from Dease Lake, to the south, touches down in a light drizzle carrying two Mounties and a physician. Despite the cold and wet, they are warmed to learn that I am safe and, to be frank, that they are spared a lengthy and grisly investigation into an aircraft accident. The chopper departs like a skittish dragonfly as quickly as it arrived, leaving me alone once again.

Only later will I learn that federal search officials had also dispatched a twin turboprop Buffalo aircraft from the Canadian Forces Base at Comox on Vancouver Island. The plane logged 2.7 hours before returning to base after news of my discovery. Officially, I became humanitarian rescue #H1726, costing about $15,000. The whole affair proved a matter of deep regret, for an experienced outdoorsman to be caught flat-footed, for the cost to the federal taxpayer, and for all the trouble and risk to which I exposed the rescue crews. It is perhaps small consolation, but the ordeal has made me a committed disciple of the doctrine that you must have a foolproof backup plan when you go into the wilderness.

By noon, a Cessna 206 floatplane piloted by Ashley Hering arrives and whisks me 130 kilometres northwest to Atlin, where I set about making arrangements for a second rescue mission: a charter flight to airlift Albrecht from the south end of Teslin Lake. I had met Albrecht perhaps three years earlier through a mutual friend in Vancouver. I cannot say I know him well, but I can tell you that he is Swiss and he is in the strange position of seeking entry to Canada as a refugee. He despises his homeland's right-wing politics, the compulsory military service, the pigeon-hole lifestyle. I know what you're thinking: "A refugee from the wealthiest per-capita country on earth? Get serious." No doubt that assessment had something to do with Canada's rejection of Albrecht's claim. But that has not stopped him. Albrecht has stayed in Canada anyway. He has a brilliant mind and he has found any number of under-the-table jobs—house renovations, artwork—almost always at well below the going wage rate. He figures if he can stay in Canada long enough and support himself, the federal government will have to grant him citizenship, and he just may be right. He shares a rental house on Commercial Drive in Vancouver, a traditionally Italian neighbourhood that has become like, cool man, anti-establishment. In an atmosphere of poets and lesbians, cappuccino and Latin folk music, the young and disenchanted sit around and complain about people who have done well for themselves.

I asked Albrecht to come north with me because he was available, because I thought he'd be good company, and because I felt he needed a break from the noxious, politically charged atmosphere of Commercial Drive. And right now I am more than a little concerned about his safety. He has never camped in the wilderness before—neither alone nor with anybody else. Moreover, he has never confronted a bear. And he has already spent one night alone in some of the most bear-infested territory in the Canadian North. I have to get him out. Fast. But Jamie Tait of Summit Air says I'll have to wait my turn this time; he has several other charters first. He expects to get around to me later this evening. In the meantime, I make the most of my time in scenic Atlin, washing my clothes at a laundromat that doubles as a library, stocking up on supplies and engaging in the sort of inane conversations that only occur in small towns so remote that the residents have lost most of their common sense.

At the restaurant, I ask, "Is there a general store in town?"

"Like for what?" the waitress replies.

"Gloves."

"One block down the street."

"What's it called?"

"The General Store."

I drop by the Atlin Inn for a rum and cola, at 7 p.m. venturing down to the dock to wait for Jamie. A native fellow returning from fishing on the Taku River asks me to help unload his catch, then gives me half a dozen pieces of smoked salmon. Delicious. By 7:40 Jamie is ready to go, though he's not keen on it. The light is fading, and his chances of making it back to Atlin before nightfall are marginal. But I figure Albrecht has already filled his pants several times by now. I pressure Jamie to leave.

As we motor away from the wharf, using First Island as a break-water, he reflects on the day's events. When he got the early-morning call from the search-and-rescue centre, officials were guessing that I might be a small aircraft that had flown to Telegraph Creek the previous day without filing a flight plan. "We had several hits on you yesterday, including from a Japanese airliner," he explains. "I got the call this morning at 5:30. The satellite gives a latitude and longitude but is not necessarily accurate—maybe within a thirty-mile radius. We dropped from 7,000 feet to 6,000 to narrow the cone of the ELT. That's when we saw your last flare."

The flight to Teslin Lake is a short one, ninety kilometres due east of Atlin over the 2,000-metre-high Teslin Plateau. En route, Jamie points out Eva Lake, a teardrop of water where he had arranged to meet a prospecting couple some years before. When they didn't show up as arranged, he notified the RCMP, as one would expect a charter pilot to do, and a search was ordered that evening. Two days later the couple were found, hiking through the bush two-thirds of the way to Trout Lake, and picked up by heli-copter. Jamie had made a couple of flights before the official search began, but the couple refused to pay his costs. "They made no effort to be found," he says bitterly. "Not even a smudge fire to be spotted, and no form of communication with them other than their not showing up and having the government go look for them." Jamie figures all hikers should carry a portable radio into the wilderness, but that's wishful thinking when it weighs two kilograms or so. And while he doesn't come out and say so directly, he thinks I'm a fool for having attempted to walk the Teslin Trail alone and squandered taxpayers' money in the process. He is entitled to his opinion. His perspective is that of a good pilot who has the opportunity to pore over a prearranged checklist every day before he goes anywhere or does anything. The rest of us do not always enjoy that luxury in our lives. Life carries a certain risk. And, of course, risk carries a price. But I am satisfied I did as much as possible to research the trail in advance and prepare myself for the trip. I am equally confident that the country is full of people who develop heart trouble from eating too much or lung cancer from smoking too much or head injuries from driving too fast and thereby cost the taxpayer far more than I did in emergency trailside assistance. If I am a fool, so be it. It was, after all, the flight of fools a century ago that lured me down the Teslin Trail in the first place. I am in good company.

As we approach our destination—the point at which the Teslin River flows into the southern extremity of Teslin Lake—I look straight down from the passenger window and spot a tiny blue tent and a white canoe marooned on a sand island in the middle of some of the finest salmon and bear habitat in the country. Oh my Lord, Albrecht, are you down there? Are you alive? Jamie splashes down in the river and gently taxis toward the island until the shallow water forces him to beach the aircraft. I jump out, run down the sandbar and motion to Albrecht. Minutes later he arrives in the canoe, but without his gear. After a big bear hug, he begins to babble. "Bears!" he shouts. "Freakin' bears!" Many bears. Bears that go thump in the night. Bears that make you long for the Alps, their goats and cows and their placid domesticity.

But there is no time to delay. The light is fading. Having performed enough rescues for one day, Jamie is anxious to leave for the town of Teslin, still a good eighty kilometres away to the north-west. We quickly paddle back to collect Albrecht's belongings, fold up the tent, and put out Albrecht's, ahem, campfire. Hell, I'm surprised we don't have to call the volunteer fire department for this one. This is no campfire; this is a towering inferno. Smokey the Bear himself would run in terror from this blast furnace and with good reason. Last night, while Albrecht was resting in his sleeping bag around 3 a.m., he felt the sand move beneath the tent. Looking outside to investigate, he found himself nose to nose with a black bear. Nobody had told Albrecht not to keep onions in his backpack in his tent. Nobody felt it was necessary. With one hand he jabbed the bear in the belly with a burning piece of log, with the other he sprayed a can of Deep Woods Off in its face. Sure, the bear left... only to return a few minutes later with its smaller buddy as backup. By this time Albrecht was breathing new life into the fire, piling it skyhigh with deadwood until it resembled the altar for some sort of aboriginal rite. Since then he had not moved far from the fire. He didn't have to. Summoned by spawning salmon, nature came to him: a family of river otters, a lynx, and just thirty minutes before my arrival, a young grizzly bear beating the bushes on the near shore. "Am I glad to see you," he confides, arm around my shoulders. "One more night and they would have gotten me."

The author's Swiss paddling partner, Albrecht, cooks up a fresh arctic grayling with a dash of spice and whiskey during the first night's camp on the Teslin River. (Larry Pynn)

8

THE TESLIN RIVER

Oh, how quickly the beguiling waters of Teslin Lake can turn treacherous. One moment the surface undulates as slowly as molten lead or glistens like polished glass, convincing us that we are paddling into the clouds. The next moment winds whip up deathly cold whitecaps like bowling balls that threaten to swamp our canoe. Beating a diagonal retreat to the shoreline, we recall that we are not the first to be threatened by these unpredictable waters.

Teslin Lake loomed as one of the most dangerous hazards faced by gold seekers on the all-Canadian Stikine Route. With its name derived from the Yukon Indian word for "long, narrow water," the lake is officially 125 kilometres long, but it all depends on where you believe the Teslin River stops and the lake begins. Because the lake narrows at both ends, local residents prefer a figure closer to 145 kilometres. Whatever the case, Teslin Lake is an indisputable monster, even by Northern standards, at an average 3 kilometres wide and 58 metres deep and draining some 28,500 square kilometres, including 5 major tributaries: the Nisutlin, Morley, Swift, Upper Teslin and Gladys rivers.

Nevertheless, it would have been easy for the Klondikers to underestimate Teslin Lake, especially if the day was calm and sunny and they were anxious to reach Dawson City. The lake must have loomed like an oasis, signalling that the worst of the hardships was over and it would be all downhill from here. Not a bad metaphor: for some, like the Chilcotin rancher Norman Lee, it was the end of the line. When Lee arrived at Teslin Lake late in 1898, he slaughtered what remained of his emaciated herd of two hundred cattle, loaded the meat onto wooden scows and set sail for Dawson just as winter was settling in. On the third day out, disaster struck. A storm blew up, the scows began to take water and the crews steered for the rocky shore to save themselves. "In a few minutes one scow was broken in two, and the other had its side and end torn off," Lee wrote, watching his investment sink. "It was not much use to save the beef...."

During the Klondike rush, prospectors emerged from the Teslin Trail at the south end of the lake at a small settlement that included a Hudson's Bay Company store, a saw mill, a shipyard, and dozens of tents and makeshift log cabins. Miners found prices for food supplies exorbitant at Teslin Lake, about forty cents a pound more than at Glenora—yet another cruel blow on their tortuous journey to the goldfields. Most of the prospectors fashioned crude wooden vessels out of the shoreline timber and set out on their journey to Dawson as soon as possible. One of the more unique modes of transport was claimed by Arthur Saint Cyr. Having arrived at Teslin Lake after twenty-six days on the Teslin Trail, his party uncrated and pieced together three folding, flat-bottomed canvas boats, each sixteen feet long and capable of carrying two men and 1,500 pounds of cargo.

As usual, the Yukon Field Force went relatively first class at the expense of the lowly prospector. On the Stikine River, the military had occupied the best camping spots; on the Teslin Trail, it had hogged the pack trains and inflated freight prices; and at Teslin Lake, it commandeered the *Anglican*, the Canadian Development Company's newly completed steamboat. "Had the Militia Department sent an official ahead of the force to confer with the Hudson Bay Co., secure all essential information and make adequate transportation arrangements, considerable friction and delay would have been prevented," concluded *Globe* correspondent Faith Fenton.

Although the steamboat *Anglican* was hired to transport an advance party of the Yukon Field Force to Fort Selkirk, most of the soldiers navigated the Teslin River on sail-equipped rowboats and scows they had crafted from the lakeshore trees. Those were exciting days for Private Lester—eating fresh moose, waterfowl and fish, riding the clear, swift-flowing river, and admiring the ever-changing Northern scenery. Even the repeated groundings on sandbars and the near-capsizing of the scows couldn't dampen his newfound sense of enthusiasm. Describing one such incident, he wrote: "Then the fun began; all hands had to tumble overboard, up to our waists in ice-cold water, and pull and haul for about twenty minutes, till at last we swung clear and went on our way, damp but rejoicing."

As the Teslin Trail fell into disuse after the Klondike rush, the Hudson's Bay trading post closed and the community of Teslin resettled farther up the lake at a more central point, Nisutlin Bay, in 1903. Today Teslin is known as Mile 804 on the Alaska Highway running between Dawson Creek, British Columbia, and Delta Junction, a hundred miles inside the Alaska border. Teslin's 500 or so residents are predominantly descendants of coastal Tlinget Indians who made their way inland to trade furs with the newly arrived Russians in the eighteenth century. For those early aboriginal nomads, Teslin Lake provided not just the fur-bearing animals necessary for the fur trade but a banquet of seasonal food: moose larger than anywhere else in North America, waters teeming with eleven species of fish, including whitefish, trout, pike, inconnu, chinook and chum salmon, and a forest heavy with fruit—wild strawberries, gooseberries, cranberries, rose hips and soapberries, which can be whipped with water and sugar to make Indian ice cream.

By mid-afternoon of our first day of paddling, food is on our minds, too. Nothing as romantic as living off the land, mind you, but something far more compelling: the famous homemade cinnamon buns of Johnson's Crossing, at the north end of the lake. I can envisage them now: soft steamy mounds erupting with sweet volcanic icing. But getting there is no easy task. We must constantly fight the temptation to take the arrow-straight shortcut across each dent in the corrugated shoreline. To do so would leave us vulnerable to the lethal vagaries of Teslin Lake.

Southern paddlers, accustomed to warmer, more forgiving waters, can be easy prey to a cold northern lake. One story I covered four years earlier for the Vancouver *Sun* still burns in my memory: the deaths of four young geologists on Tatsamenie Lake, west of Dease Lake, on a mining expedition. All were in their early twenties and physically fit, a fact that cruelly worked against them. With little body fat, they had no natural insulation against the deadly cold water. When their canoe flipped, it didn't take long before they became hypothermic, their limbs went numb, and with no hope of swimming to shore, they all drowned.

Albrecht and I plan not to make the same mistake. After a couple of close calls of our own, we hug the shoreline religiously, taking the opportunity to practise our paddling techniques under safe conditions before we enter the Teslin River at Johnson's Crossing. We quickly discover that paddling flat water can be monotonous and frustrating, especially when you have no time to waste. Because of delays on the Teslin Trail (a late start from Telegraph Creek, cleaning up Fletcher's cabin, getting rescued), I am behind schedule and in no position to extend my trip. Therefore our task is written in stone—eleven days to canoe the remaining eight hundred kilometres to Dawson, a sizzling pace for any canoeist, leaving us no margin for error.

As we plough methodically along the shore with a strong head wind resisting our passage, Albrecht begins to appreciate the magnitude of our undertaking. And I begin to discover the subtleties of my partner's personality. When conditions are good and the weather fine, he is a warm, rollicking tailwind—full of cheer, jokes and challenging, insightful conversation. But his mood changes as easily as the northern weather. When the going gets tough, Albrecht can become consumed with negativity and self-doubt. I in turn begin to question my choice of travelling partner, as many a prospector a century earlier must have. But the die is cast. The Klondike lies ahead. Albrecht, let's pick up the pace.

Our gruelling fifty-kilometre paddle from Teslin to Johnson's Crossing takes twelve hours. Although occasionally tedious, the trip is not without its moments: a cow moose, splashing in the water on the far shore, seeking respite from the torment of mosquitoes; loons diving through the cold clear waters for fish; the ever-changing clouds, big and dark and scary as they spin off the top of the Yukon Plateau and unfold in enormous billows over the lake; the necklace of small homesteads dotting the shoreline next to the Alaska Highway. Albrecht recognizes one of them, a half-finished log house owned by a native man who gave him a ride when he was hitchhiking to Teslin for our rendezvous. The native and his friends smoked dope and drank with Albrecht and even offered to take him hunting, Yukon style: driving up and down the road with a loaded rifle, ready to kill the first moose to step out of the bush. He declined.

At its northern extremity, Teslin Lake begins to narrow and the current slowly builds momentum. It is imperceptible until you look down and see the water plants streaming across the lake bottom, all pointing the same way. Just ahead is Johnson's Crossing, officially named after Colonel Frank Johnson of the U.S. Army Engineers, builders of the steel bridge across the Teslin River during construction of the Alaska Highway. Teslin residents have their own version. Ignoring the subtle difference in spelling, they claim the bridge was named after George Johnston, a Tlingit Indian who became known for his photography of native culture and, even more prominently, as owner of the community's first car, a 1928 four-door Chevy sedan purchased new from Taylor and Drury's garage in Whitehorse for $1,172.50. Johnston had the car delivered aboard the steamboat *Thistle* for use as a taxi service. With no Alaska Highway to drive on, he cut a swath through the shoreline forest for a road and in winter had the run of the frozen lake, charging residents anywhere from one to fifteen dollars, depending on the distance. During winter hunting trips, he would drain the water from the radiator and keep it warm over the campfire until he'd shot his game. If a tire went flat away from the village, he'd patch it up with moose hide and hobble home. And if he drove on the ice too close to spring breakup, he'd ditch the vehicle on the lakefront and pick it up later with a boat and outboard motor. The car, affectionately known as Sonny, was eventually bought back by Charlie Taylor for $750 in 1962.

At 539 metres, the steel bridge at Johnson's Crossing is the third-longest span on the Alaska Highway and built high enough to accommodate the riverboats that used to ply the river, bringing supplies from Whitehorse to remote Teslin. As it turned out, transportation improved so drastically with completion of the highway that there was little need for the slower and costlier riverboats. The trend would be repeated on the Yukon River with completion of the Klondike Highway between Dawson and Whitehorse in 1955. Such highway projects were fine for the larger towns serviced by them, but smaller river communities left without transport had no alternative but to pack up or gradually wither on the vine.

American tourist William Reid examines a graveyard of trucks abandoned by the United States military on the Canol Road at Johnson's Crossing in southern Yukon during the final days of the Second World War. (Larry Pynn)

Albrecht and I haul out the canoe on the west bank and set up camp under the bridge like a couple of weary trolls. Johnson's Crossing, a combination of store, gas stop and café, is just a few steps away, but the true object of our interest lies across the river, hidden from motorists travelling the Alaska Highway. Buried among the overgrown bushes is one of the most interesting, if neglected, historic sites in the Yukon: a graveyard of old military vehicles abandoned by the U.S. government in the last days of the Second World War.

On the evening we arrive at Johnson's Crossing, precious little light can be squeezed from the northern sun. But I will not be deterred. Not this close. Gathering up William Reid, an elderly American tourist awaiting engine repairs to his motor home, we strike out for the wrecking yard: over the Teslin River bridge; up the Canol Road, part of the American military oil-supply route that ran almost a thousand kilometres from the oil town of Norman Wells, Northwest Territories, to a refinery in Whitehorse; then a sharp left turn behind a thicket of alders. Upon arrival, we are surprised by the number of rusting, olive-coloured trucks—battered, bruised and half-gutted shells, stripped of their dignity but laid out in neat rows like crosses in a military cemetery. To walk among the ghosts of these Yukon road warriors and sit on old springs behind a steering wheel is fun, yes, but also a little unsettling. With his craggy features, grey beard, leather work boots and torn blue coverall, Reid does not look the least bit out of place. When he pushes aside the encroaching brush and swaggers up to one of the vehicles, you half expect him to pop the hood, roll up his sleeves and exclaim, "I told you boys not to work these rigs so hard. Now look at the work you've created for me."

The next morning, we greet our chosen route to the Klondike with renewed enthusiasm. For the next two hundred kilometres, we finally have the smooth flow of the Teslin River to add vigour to our paddling and an ever-changing landscape to heighten our curiosity. Through the clear depths of about four metres beneath our canoe, blood-red spawning salmon waft lazily over pristine gravel beds. Farther downstream, they break the surface with a loud cannonading splash, catching the eye of marauding ravens and bald eagles. From our left, a small, motorized punt approaches bearing two hunters, each as unflinching as the moose corpse at their feet. Later, we spot two men on the raised riverbank, staring intently at a marsh across the river. One man wears camouflage green, the other a red wool sweater, binoculars slung around his neck. Albrecht waves twice as we approach but there is no response. Just two grumpy stone faces. "Hunting?" Albrecht asks innocently.

"Yes," one of them replies.

"Sorry. Good luck." To which the other man, presumably a German paying thousands of dollars for a wilderness hunt, grunts animal-like and resumes his stare.

It is at this point that I begin to perceive another aspect of Albrecht's personality: his disdain for Germans. The Swiss view of Germans is not unexpected and not very different from that of any people forced to endure a louder, larger neighbour—the relationship, say, between Canadians and Americans or Finns and Swedes. But I am still surprised by the depth of Albrecht's feelings. At the start of our trip, I had informed Albrecht that residents of Dawson say there are two ways to canoe the Yukon River, with the synchronized precision of a German drill team, or with Canadian affability, feet draped over the gunwale, a beer in one hand and a paddle in the other. Albrecht chose the latter image, insisting that he had abandoned the Swiss way of thinking. And for the most part he had. But all it took to inflame his patriotic competitiveness was the sight of a German paddling ahead on the river. There could be no relaxing until that canoe had been overtaken and its paddlers left choking on our frothy wake.

We choose a campsite that night beside a deep, clear canyon dominated by hoodoo gravel formations, just upstream of the Swift River. The churning carcasses of spawned-out salmon float past our tent, soon to run aground on sandbars and be devoured by patrolling bears. I am more interested in the arctic grayling, a small whitefish with a distinctive flared dorsal fin that is said to be easily caught—just how easy I am about to find out. Having somehow lost my fishing rod in the airline luggage transfer between Seattle and Anchorage, I am forced to make do with, well, my camera tripod. No, I wouldn't make it on the *American Sportsman* TV program, but, hey, who am I impressing? A Swiss who uses bug spray on bears? I unfold the device to its maximum extension, tie a line and spinner to the end, and let fly across the still surface. Almost instantly, I feel a strong tug. Then another. And then the real thing. No finesse here. I give the line a strong yank, and the grayling is mine, flopping around helplessly on the rocks. Now Albrecht takes over. As designated chef for the trip, he is above beans and wieners. With a hint of spices and a splash of Jack Daniels, he produces a restaurant-quality dinner just as dusk settles over our camp.

The Teslin River begins slow and meandering, a big fish tail gently slicing its way through the land, then settles into a pattern of moderate currents followed by swollen pools, as though the river had a capacity for breathing. With each passing kilometre, the river picks up steam, but also loses its lustre. The wind snaps its fingers and curls of dust dance off the steep eroded banks that dominate both sides of the river, befouling the water to the point where you can actually hear the grit rasp against the canoe.

By late afternoon we approach the Boswell River, named after Thomas and George Boswell, two brothers from Ontario who prospected this region as far back as the early 1880s. Roaming Alaska and the Yukon with the freedom of wild animals, sniffing out one stream after another, these two shared in the first gold discoveries on the Stewart River, a major tributary of the Yukon upstream of Dawson. Thomas would eventually pay the penalty for his lifestyle, losing a leg in an attack by a grizzly in 1891. But having paved the way for the Klondike gold rush, he didn't allow his injury to stop him from joining in when the big strike happened. Near the riverbank remains an old log cabin with a sod roof and dirt floor, chicken wire over the windows, and a low bed with a moss mattress. It would be great to camp here with the Boswells' ghosts, sucking up the warm sun on a sandy beach, but there is still too much daylight and too much river to travel. Lamentably, no matter how much time I allocate for a wilderness trip, I always come up short.

Just downstream the Roaring Bull Rapids await us—not rapids, per se, but just enough fast water to raise your adrenaline level and leave you craving more. Alas, neither the Teslin nor the Yukon is a white-water river. Miles Canyon and the White Horse Rapids, on the Yukon at Whitehorse, were once threats to river-boaters but have since been silenced by the building of hydro dams. Only the historic Five Finger Rapids, upstream of Dawson on the Yukon, still offer any semblance of adventure. The fact is that although both the Teslin and the Yukon are capable of a respectable, even a blistering pace, they pose little danger to mod-ern-day boaters using common sense. To canoe them requires more grunt force than finesse. Of course, one benefit of such a journey is a nice slow troll. I check the fishing line dangling off the back of the canoe around mid-day, and yahoo! Another grayling.

Thirty kilometres downstream on the left bank is O'Brien's Bar, the first evidence of a gold-mining operation on the Teslin River. Most of the mining along the Teslin and Yukon occurred up the smaller tributaries and well away from the main rivers. But these particular works sit exposed on the riverbank for all to see, weather-beaten, rusted, and still resisting the northern elements. Beside them is an old barge and behind it is a series of deep trenches and a tailing pile of rocks. All are devoid of plant life, the earth and gravel that were the lifeblood having been sucked out. In the background, spruce trees grow on the dirt floor of an old cabin, and strewn all around are old pipes, pumps and machinery, one piece stamped "San Francisco."

Fewer than ten kilometres along we reach Teslin Crossing, midway point on a winter trail that ran west to east from Lake Laberge on the Yukon River system to Livingstone, a mining community at the mouth of Livingstone Creek that flourished for several years and is claimed to have produced more than a million dollars in gold in the years following the Klondike strike. All is quiet at Teslin Crossing, essentially a former ferry-crossing point, when Albrecht and I pull ashore just below a trapper's cabin on the left bank. The place is covered with blue and orange tarps, and a sign posted by the Yukon territorial government on a stump warns that the area may be mined with traps. "Use at your own risk," it says, asking visitors to respect the livelihood of others. But it falls a good deal short of being a no-trespassing sign. We walk inside the cabin and snoop around. The place boasts a transistor radio tuned to the CBC, a woodstove, a propane lamp and a bed littered with magazines—*Guns and Ammo, Guns, Hunting*—and the Vancouver *Sun* for February 25, 1991, headlined "Land, air, sea strikes drive for Kuwait City." Judging by this man's reading material, I'm just as happy he's not home.

Longing to stretch our legs, we take a fifteen-minute hike to a cemetery on a dry bluff above the cabin. The inspiring view of the river and, farther to the east, the Big Salmon Range of the Pelly Mountains is worth the effort. The cemetery, however, yields few clues. A wooden picket fence around the grave sites is in varying degrees of disrepair, and most of the names are either missing or worn off. But from death comes life: spruce and aspen trees rise up from the fertile soil. A better headstone a Klondiker could not ask.

Up to this point, Albrecht and I have been spoiled. Since leaving Johnson's Crossing, we have met no other travellers, have not had to share the river and its historic sites with anyone. All that is about to change; we are about to discover that foreigners continue to dominate the route to the goldfields. A century ago Americans swamped the Yukon in their search for untold riches. Today the influx is European tourists, mainly Germans raised on the century-old, swashbuckling outdoor writings of Karl May, Germany's answer to Jack London. These modern visitors know a little of the history of the Klondike. They are seeking, however, something far more valuable and elusive than gold: a wilderness experience no longer possible in a country three-quarters the size of the Yukon and populated by eighty million people. They want the adventure that many Canadians take for granted.

Fifteen kilometres downstream, two canoes rest on the shore. We pull ashore and shout hello. Again, but still no response. The owners would probably just as soon be left alone. Too bad. Here we come. Scrambling up the clay embankment, we spot a neat camp with two tents, pots hanging from stands, and two couples. Very efficient. Very German. As we approach their campsite, Albrecht quietly recommends that I remove my sunglasses. It's the European way. The four travellers, from the Frankfurt area, are on the twenty-second day of their journey. After motoring up the Canol Road, they launched their canoes on the Nisutlin River and floated downriver to Teslin before following the same route that we had. They are now headed for the community of Carmacks on the Yukon River before returning home. "This is my tenth trip to

Canada, mostly the Yukon," explains Brigitte Brauch, a travel agent with the best English in the group. "I have paddled the Big Salmon River and Pelly River." With canoes rented in Whitehorse, the four are travelling late in the season to avoid the crowds. So far, so good: fishing for grayling's a snap, and just one day of rain. "It's so beautiful. We don't like going to Spain or Italy."

A short paddle and we arrive at Mason Landing, presumably named after the trapper and prospector brothers Willoughby and Reuben Mason. The settlement served as both a steamboat landing and a supply centre, connecting with Livingstone mining camp by a wagon road. In its prime, Mason Landing boasted not just the riverboat stop but also a roadhouse and stable, a telegraph station, and a small trading post. A century later the place still makes for an interesting walk. One cabin with a roof of wooden poles is in surprisingly good shape. Inside, old gasoline cans are flattened and tacked to the wall to provide a heat guard for the wood-stove. Other cabins are in more perilous shape. Anything for a photograph: Albrecht cannot resist poking his head through a stovepipe hole in a decaying roof. Pulling it out is another matter, a slow, painful process; but gradually he works himself free, rust stains dribbling down his face like tears.

Another thirty kilometres downstream, near the North West Mounted Police post of Hootalinqua (an aboriginal word for "river running against the mountain"), the Teslin's murky waters merge with the blue of the mighty Yukon River. History melds here, too; prospectors who had followed the all-Canadian route up the Stikine River, over the Teslin Trail and down the Teslin River merged with the much greater flood of miners who had taken the main Klondike routes overland via the Chilkoot and White Pass trails and then by boat down the Yukon River. Anxious to complete their journey, the Teslin River prospectors must have viewed the Yukon River as a positive sign that they were one step closer to their destination. As for Albrecht and me, we leave the serene and relatively untravelled Teslin with mixed feelings, wondering if our sense of intimacy with the landscape and its history will be diminished along the busier Yukon River. As it turns out, we are simply shifting gears. With a strong thrust of the paddles, we plough into the main stream of the Yukon River and aim for Hootalinqua. Full steam ahead, Albrecht!

Brightly painted fencing, this one at Fork Selkirk, is typical
of native Indian cemeteries found along the Yukon River.
(Larry Pynn)

9

THE SMELL OF BANNOCK

"What is it, schnitzel?" I innocently ask Stefanie Ritz and Stephan Schusser, frying up lunch at a riverfront picnic table below Hootalinqua.

"No, bannock," Stephan replies. In case there is any doubt, he holds up a recipe from a German guidebook on canoeing in Canada. Canadians, apparently, don't venture into the wilderness without a healthy supply of bannock. And if Germans want both to blend in with the locals and become one with the environment, they've gotta have bannock. The rest of us know you stand a much better chance of finding a Canadian camper with a case of beer than a batch of bannock, but why spoil the image? After all, this couple may have been practising for months. I smear some peanut butter on a piece and try a bite. Not bad, actually, but it still looks like schnitzel.

Stefanie and Stephan are your basic slack-asses: up at 9 a.m., on the river by 2 p.m. I am jealous. Albrecht and I have no time to waste in our eleven-day quest for Dawson. We're becoming a lean, mean paddling machine. In fact, we're starting to act more German than the Germans. This particular couple, having learned about the Yukon from friends back in Munich, are paddling from Whitehorse to Carmacks with virtually no canoeing experience. They tell us about the bald eagles and the mosquitoes and all those huge sand cliffs viewed en route. Sure, they were appalled that the city of Whitehorse releases its sewage into the Yukon, but that didn't stop them from bathing in the river. The biggest surprise, however, has been the company they've kept on the river—other German tourists. They are finding them around almost every bend. All reading the same guidebook. All munching on bannock. "It's disappointing," confides Stefanie, gradually accepting the fact that her countrymen are attracted to Canada for the same reasons she is. "It's the space, the outdoors. We come from a small country. Not at all wild."

They have had a practical problem, too. Their canoe, rented in Whitehorse at twenty-five dollars a day, is leaking. Lake Laberge proved especially troublesome, with high winds, slow paddling, heavy bailing. Perhaps their troubles are over. One could seek no better place to effect repairs than Hootalinqua, a former shipyard. One look at my mangy wool pants gives us the solution: duct tape. Albrecht tears several strips off the roll with his teeth and attaches them to the bow of their canoe, only too eager to illustrate the superiority of the Swiss over the Germans.

Because of its strategic position just below the confluence of the Yukon and Teslin rivers, Hootalinqua once served as a fishing camp for Yukon Indians intercepting salmon on one of the longest spawning migrations in the world, more than 3,000 kilometres from the Bering Sea on Alaska's west coast to the upper Teslin River. As prospectors began trickling into this region in the mid-1880s, Hootalinqua became a natural supply post and expanded with the Klondike gold discovery into a riverboat landing, outpost for the North West Mounted Police, a telegraph station, and a winter shipyard.

The first thing I notice about Hootalinqua is the good condition of the buildings, newly roofed and log walls chinked with concrete for longevity. One cabin is wedged into the hillside like a badger. Inside, muffin trays and rolls of wire are hung neatly on the walls. A frying pan still sits on the stove, as though the cook has just gone out back to the two-hole shitter. Unlike the historic gold-rush sites along the Teslin River, Hootalinqua shows few signs of modern garbage or land mines, our euphemism for human excrement left along trails in the bush. There are even signs posted warning that the removal of archaeological specimens is punishable by a maximum fine of $1,000 and/or one year in jail under the Yukon Act, a reflection of the government's commitment to preserve the memory of the Klondike on this, the most important route to Dawson. The irony is that we found no such signs along the Teslin River, where the government is more interested in preserving the property rights of a trapper fascinated by macho magazines than the last evidence of the major all-Canadian route to the goldfields.

Just downstream are the historic shipyards of Hootalinqua Island, built by the British Yukon Navigation Company in 1913. Vessels requiring winter storage were hauled up greased wooden skidways by a cable wrapped around the hull. Horses slowly turned four capstans that wound up the cable and hoisted the ship into

Have family will travel, John and Bev Morrison and their three children, shown next to the old shipyards of Hootalinqua Island, are Yukoners whose idea of a summer holiday is paddling the historic Yukon River. (Larry Pynn)

place. Then it was levelled and blocked up, safe from the onslaught of river ice. Today the island is dominated by the hulking skeletal remains of the 360-tonne stern-wheeler *Evelyn*. Built about 1908 for trade on the lower Yukon River in Alaska, the vessel was bought by a Canadian company in 1913 and renamed *Norcom*. It travelled from Whitehorse to the Bering Sea for just one season before it was abandoned at Hootalinqua and its machinery salvaged, pre-

sumably for use on another vessel. At Hootalinqua Island, there is
not even a pretense of a government heritage site. The *Evelyn* is
collapsing upon itself, rotting away with all the grace and dignity
of a beached whale.

On the riverfront beneath the ship is something equally curious—a family of five, belongings strewn across the sandy beach,
ready to be crammed into a single 5.5-metre canoe. You'd think
five passengers would be more than enough—John and Bev
Morrison and their children, Troy, thirteen, Tanya, six, and Adam,
five—but apparently not. They are expecting to pick up one more
burly traveller along the way: a moose. John carries a 30-06 rifle
in hopes of bagging one on the shore and taking it home for the
winter meat supply. What, no bannock? And you call yourselves
Canadians? The Morrisons left Whitehorse four days earlier and
have allowed another twelve days to reach Dawson. Despite the
five-horsepower outboard motor attached to their canoe, they
took two days to cross Lake Laberge. John is reluctant to call
the trip a holiday for his children. It is damned hard work, a
wilderness experience and a hands-on lesson in Canadian history.
But a holiday? Don't tell his kids. "I really like it," says Troy, joining in. "All the historical stuff. We passed lower Laberge—old
cabins and a telegraph base and the hull of a ship and a trapline.
It was really neat."

I notice that Bev is deliberately keeping quiet in the background,
continuing the chore of packing up camp. Then it strikes me: I
know this woman! No, wait. I've interviewed her before, almost a
year earlier, at her homestead west of Whitehorse as part of an
advance series for the Vancouver *Sun* on the fiftieth anniversary

of the Alaska Highway. As a Yukon Indian and member of the Champagne-Aishihik band, Bev had spoken critically of natives who hold out for land claims and government handouts rather than making their own way in the world. Band leaders hadn't liked her comments, which only confirmed what was on the minds of many white people, and they let her know it. "They only printed the bad stuff," Bev recalls, too polite to ask if that was all I had reported.

"She got into shit," John, a red scarf wrapped pirate-style around his head, confirms with a smile. "At least they know what she thinks now." For me, the coincidence of meeting the same person twice in less than a year and under such unlikely conditions is unsettling. Is it really as small a world as people suggest? Or after twenty years in journalism, is there no one new left for me to interview?

The Morrison family leaves first, but we soon overtake them, paddling in a light drizzle. Then the Germans, Stefanie and Stephan, pop up out of nowhere, hugging the left inside bank on a turn in the river while we follow the main current in a wide arc to the outside. As they push ahead of us, Albrecht is not amused and is beginning to blame me. As the one with the topo maps and controlling the steering, I must be more careful not to let others get ahead of us. After all, this is war! But I am not interested in fighting age-old ethnic battles. Besides, whatever happened to the neutral Swiss? The difficulty is that with every passing kilometre the Yukon River sucks up more tributaries and becomes increasingly bloated, eventually fanning out into a complex series of channels and islands. It is a full-time job to know your exact position on the map at any given moment and ensure you take the channel most likely to give you maximum velocity. I am not into it; after all, it's not as though

Twin waterfalls pour off a mountain side into the Yukon River, an ever-changing landscape that attracts wilderness canoeists from all over the world. (Larry Pynn)

we are in any danger of getting lost. All the major landmarks—the incoming rivers, the historic sites, the larger mountains—have been obvious when we reached them. I prefer to go with the flow, with a minimum of effort.

Albrecht and I are having other differences. I find his negativity grating. For me, a cloudy day foretells sunny weather. For

Albrecht, it is a sure sign of rain and head winds. I had hoped that time in the wilderness, away from the cynicism of East End Vancouver coffee bars, would give Albrecht a new lease on life. I was wrong; you can take the man out of Commercial Drive, but you cannot take Commercial Drive out of the man. There is, however, nothing novel about our predicament—certainly not on this river and certainly not among men who go for the gold. Indeed, partners carried on some horrific feuds during the gold rush. One of the most outrageous of such stories emerged at the Big Salmon River, just ahead of us. Ten partners reportedly became so disgusted with each other that they divided their holdings into ten parts on ten blankets, including the splinters of a big wooden scow, each preferring to build his own transport out of the remains to venturing one more kilometre downriver together. In the historical perspective, maybe we aren't doing so badly, after all. There has not been a single discussion of sawing our fibreglass canoe in half. And I can still bring a smile to a Swiss face. On a relatively straight stretch of river near Cassiar Bar, we pour the steam to the pipes and rocket past Stefanie and Stephan. "Yahoo, Albrecht! Hang on while I get the water skis!" At Big Salmon River, we pull ashore to explore the historic site several minutes ahead of them, watching as they get stuck in the mud several metres from the riverbank. An embarrassing predicament, and such a neat canoe, too. Stefanie looks up and launches her best broadside salvo: "Your canoe is such a mess." Yes, but it is not patched with duct tape.

A party of four prospectors first explored the Big Salmon River, the Yukon tributary named by Indians living nearby, in 1881, travelling some three hundred kilometres upstream of the mouth and becoming the first producing gold miners in the Yukon. Pacing through the remains of the settlement at the confluence a century later, I smell—no, it couldn't be—bannock? Two Germans from Freiburg, Rolf Schurr, an air-conditioning technician, and his architect companion, Franz Kiermeir, have taken over one of the old cabins as their personal roadhouse and are frying a pizza-like substance over a campfire. A sign erected by the Tsawlyjik Dan First Nation reads, "May the spirits travel with you," and provides an interesting counterpoint to the row of empty liquor bottles inside the cabin—Glenfiddich, Ballantine's—evidence of the well-heeled modern traveller. With Albrecht acting as interpreter, the two Germans describe a most harrowing experience, a canoe trip that began two weeks ago on Quiet Lake, near the Canol Road about sixty kilometres north of Johnson's Crossing. The two friends had been planning their trip meticulously for three years. But there are some things you cannot plan for, some things you cannot antici-pate. Call it Deliverance, Black Forest style. "Very difficult—low water, big boulders and sharp turns," says Rolf, mentioning merely in passing close sightings of a grizzly and a wolf. "We hit a boulder in a rapid and flipped out. Franz grabbed the canoe, but I was swept to the other side of the river. For two hours I looked for a place to cross. Eventually I went upstream one or two hundred metres. We lost both paddles and had only one spare. So we had to use a branch, but we found the other paddle in an eddy two kilometres downstream. It was pretty wild." So who says there's no adventure left in the North?

With the arrival of Stefanie and Stephan this place is starting to feel crowded. Despite the late hour, Albrecht and I press on down the river, passing an old log cabin teetering on the lip of the riverbank adorned with a Block Brothers for sale sign. A little wilderness humour. Seventeen kilometres below Big Salmon, we appropriate a historic campsite of our own: Cyr's Dredge, on the right bank. In 1940, Laurent Cyr and Boyd Gordon built a dredge in Whitehorse from a stripped-down Cat tractor, a car engine and a variety of homemade parts and floated it downriver for a summer's gold mining. In the hit-and-run style that typifies mining even today, the men took seventy-two ounces of fine gold from the river in twenty days, then abandoned the entire operation.

Although the mechanical bucket-dredge dates back to New Zealand in 1867, the first dredges didn't flex their muscles in the Yukon until after the initial Klondike gold rush. In 1899, Cassiar Bar got the first one, which was later moved to Bonanza Creek near Dawson. Because of their ability to process huge amounts of gravel in a short period, dredges excelled in speed and efficiency. They profitably reworked placer sites that had been abandoned by prospectors relying on manual labour to dig through the muck and frozen gravel. But in the process these dredges exacted a heavy environmental toll, strip-mining the landscape and turning prime salmon-spawning streams into barren backwaters. Even today, nothing grows on the dead zone of rock tailings left by these operations.

Over the years, thirty-five dredges were built in the Yukon, the last of them operating well into the 1950s. Perhaps the most famous, forty-three-metre No. 4 dredge, was powered by the hydro plant the Yukon Consolidated Gold Corporation built on the Klondike River, forty-eight kilometres away. As an example of its awesome might, during 262 days in 1939 on Hunker Creek, the dredge processed 1.3 million cubic metres of gravel and recovered almost one million grams of gold. Today, No. 4 dredge is being restored by the federal parks service on Bonanza Creek.

Yesterday's garbage is today's artifact. Unless there is money for preservation, however, there comes a point at which artifacts revert to garbage. Like the *Evelyn*, Cyr's Dredge is falling victim to the elements. Although its trommel, the large cylindrical screen used for washing the gravel, is still in pretty good shape, the dredge overall is a wreck, awaiting nature's slow but inevitable death sentence.

I awake to a light morning rain and a bit of an internal drizzle. For years I have drunk from wilderness waterways with impunity, boiling the water only under the most suspect conditions. Now I am paying the price at a time I can least afford to. After several days of giardiasis-induced diarrhea, my energy levels are noticeably waning. Everything seems fine until I eat or drink; then my intestinal response is swift and certain, violent enough to discourage me from eating at all. Not surprisingly, I am losing weight. Healthy or not, Albrecht and I must maintain an average pace of seventy-five kilometres a day to reach Dawson. Help, fortunately, is almost in sight. There is a medical station at the community of Carmacks, a day's paddle away.

Just a few minutes into our morning paddle we pass the remnants of another dredge, mired in a slough near an old woodcutters' camp. Several such camps once dotted the banks of the Yukon River, providing fuel for the Klondike's steam-driven stern-wheelers. Indeed, an estimated 150,000 to 200,000 cubic metres of wood were cut annually in the Yukon between 1898 and 1901, a figure that has not been exceeded even a century later. As I contemplate

*Abandoned log cabins with sod roofs stare back at canoeists
paddling the Teslin River, part of the century-old all-Canadian
Stikine route to the Klondike goldfields in Dawson, Yukon.*
(Larry Pynn)

the spectacle of Klondike-era clear-cutting, my eye is drawn to an
unusual piece of driftwood on the right bank. Drawn with good
reason: it is not wood at all but a cow moose, resting on the sand,
head down, nose at the water's edge, a wild-eyed look her only
sign of life. Pulling ashore just downstream, we walk back ever so
slowly to investigate. She is a pathetic sight, near death. Although

she shows no blood stains or obvious signs of injury, my guess is that she was shot by a passing boater but managed to escape into the forest. Returning now to the river's edge to die, she will find no peace in this well-travelled location. When we are ten metres away, she looks up at us, twitches her ears, rises gamely to her feet and walks unsteadily back into the forest. For such a potent symbol of the North, it is an ignoble end.

Moose sightings are not as common as you might think in the Yukon, so I count this one, as imperfect as it may be. Because of the natives' drive-by-shooting style of hunting, the Yukon's highways are pretty much swept clean of moose. Such indiscriminate hunting practices tell us more about the aboriginals' historic connection to the land than does the modern fairy-tale image of the native as conservationist. It is true that natives historically lived in harmony with their environment, but mostly because their primitive hunting methods limited their ability to catch game. Europeans altered that balance forever with the introduction of firearms and motor vehicles, which give hunters the means to travel widely and effectively over vast distances, day and night, winter and summer.

Wildlife in the Yukon took its first major hit with the influx of hungry gold seekers who had little alternative for food in the late 1800s. The caribou, an inquisitive animal and not at all wary, proved especially vulnerable to exploitation. The Fortymile caribou herd once numbered hundreds of thousands of animals over a huge area of the Yukon and Alaska, from Whitehorse and Dawson to Fairbanks and Fort Yukon. But over the past century—a period in which the caribou have gone through a series of recoveries and

Successful hunters, these Dawson residents use a block-and-tackle to hoist two bull moose up from a marsh and onto a sandbar for skinning and gutting next to the Yukon River. (Larry Pynn)

declines—the herd has been reduced to several thousand animals. Today only the most determined conservation efforts could return the herd to its former glorious numbers.

Not far downstream from our moose sighting, near the mouth of the Little Salmon River we investigate the historic native settlement of Little Salmon, abandoned following a deadly outbreak of influenza in the early 1900s. Death continues to set the tone for the place. Rows of bright, freshly painted wooden spirit houses keep watch over burial plots neatly fenced to keep out animals. Poplars around the cemetery grow exceptionally tall and strong, their roots forming natural conduits to the spirit world. Some of the houses contain personal effects that the deceased might find useful in the next world—shoes, a suitcase, a stool, a coffee pot, a table with a dish. Natives claim that the spirit of the deceased will bring bad luck to anyone who takes these objects, but the fate of countless American soldiers who plundered such burial sites during construction of the Alaska Highway remains unknown. According to native tradition, relatives throw a memorial potlatch for the deceased, a ceremony that comforts the mourners and ensures a respectful send-off for the loved one in a warm atmosphere of community sharing.

There is also plenty of evidence of current human occupation: a playground and a set of outhouses, a scatter of new cabins, a black dog guarding a white canvas tent, an old fishing boat, salmon drying on wooden racks, jackets and bicycles left outdoors. I shout hello, but no one responds: only a silky black raven, mascot to half the Yukon Indian clan members, winging its way through the settlement. Then we hear the sound of an ore truck travelling the Robert Campbell Highway, shattering the silence like cannon fire. After several days on this wilderness route, our senses have become attuned to the subtleties of nature: the crack of a twig, the wing-beat of a bird in flight, the first gentle strokes of a head wind. Now we must endure the culture shock of traffic noisily travelling from Carmacks east to the Faro lead-zinc mine and the native community of Ross River on the Canol Road. But sounds of modern civilization are at least a positive sign that medical treatment is not far off. We begin the final assault on Carmacks silently in a light shower, watching drops of rain bounce off the water's surface as if it were oil in a hot skillet.

Carmacks derives its name from George Washington Carmack, a Californian who ventured north to the Yukon, married a Tagish Indian woman, and developed a coal and trapping business here at the confluence of the Nordenskiold and Yukon rivers in the early 1890s. While the settlement he founded prospered as a riverboat stop and supply centre for mining in the region, Carmack himself went on to bigger things, sharing in the big gold strike on Rabbit (Bonanza) Creek with two Yukon natives, Dawson Charlie and Skookum Jim, on August 17, 1896. Carmack was an educated man who kept an organ and classical literature in his cabin. Unlike so many prospectors, he didn't squander all his riches and died a relatively wealthy man in Vancouver in 1922.

Carmacks comes upon us so quickly that we are under the bridge (the only crossing of the Yukon River between Whitehorse and Dawson) and past the territorial campground before we know it. Grudgingly, we paddle back upriver and pull ashore at a wet, soggy campsite. Enough of this: tonight we splurge on a hotel room. Carmacks may have only five hundred people, but for us, after so many days on the river, it possesses all the glittering allure of a Nevada gambling town. For tonight, at least, Carmacks is the Biggest Little City in the Yukon.

Albrecht and I set up a tent anyway, to make it look like someone is minding the canoe. Then we check into the Carmacks Hotel.

We take our first hot shower since Teslin, wash our filthy clothes in the laundromat, then primp ourselves for a night at the Gold Dust Lounge. Our sense of timing is perfect. The hotel chef, nicknamed Kung Fu because of his long, thin moustache, is celebrating his forty-second birthday, and his friends are about to give him his present: a stripper imported from Whitehorse. Kung Fu is enthroned on a chair in the middle of the dance floor, surrounded by colourful balloons, while the stripper teases through her routine. As I watch from the bar, I exchange pleasantries with the waitress. She taunts, "Just tell us when your birthday is, Larry."

Unfortunately, I am unable to enjoy a restful sleep on the comfortable mattress; I am up three times in the night, running to the bathroom with explosive diarrhea. In the morning, wasting no time, I visit the federal medical clinic. There are no doctors on duty, but a nurse in civilian clothes agrees to see me as a walk-in patient. I am immediately reminded of those four brave women of the Victorian Order of Nurses who left the comfort of their homes in Toronto and the Maritimes a century ago to venture north to rugged Dawson and provide medical attention where little existed. "If all patients could receive the careful nursing which is given by these devoted women," wrote Dr. J.W. Good, medical officer for Dawson in 1899, "the mortality would be substantially decreased." Of the four, Margaret Payson eventually took a job at the Dawson post office and married a wealthy miner; Amy Scott and Georgia Powell went to serve with Canadian field hospitals in South Africa; and Rachel Hanna found employment as matron of the Atlin hospital before heading overseas in the First World War.

The walls of the office are posted with information on AIDS, the latest in the series of sinister diseases that have been inflicted on northern communities over the past century. The nurse reports a flu going around town, but she says I don't exhibit the usual symptoms of aching muscles, aside from what would be caused by paddling up to one hundred kilometres a day. She agrees with my diagnosis of giardia and gives me a free, seven-day supply of 250-mg Flagyl tablets. "No alcohol or you'll really get sick," she adds. The comment only serves to remind me that my nicotine-addicted paddling partner has traded away the last of my Jack Daniels for cigarettes from the two Germans at Big Salmon. In return, one day I will replace his precious Swiss chocolate with Milk Duds.

Back in our canoe and pulling away from Carmacks, we wave to a group of school children who are walking along the shore picking up garbage that has drifted downstream from who knows where. Out on a limb, a mature bald eagle dries its wings and watches warily as our canoe passes below. But I take its presence as a good omen. Some thirty-four kilometres downstream of Carmacks awaits Five Finger Rapids, the only significant white water on our journey, created by four large rock outcrops situated in mid-river. At the site of an abandoned coal mine, just above the rapids on the right bank, Albrecht and I pull ashore for what he calls an anxiety pee. Tie-downs for the waterproof plastic pails containing our provisions are double checked to ensure they won't work free in the event the canoe flips. Although the Five Finger Rapids are a relatively minor threat to today's manoeuvrable canoe, they represented a potentially serious obstacle to gold seekers a century

The Five Finger Rapids, named because of the large rocks in midstream of the Yukon River, were one of the obstacles faced by miners en route to the Klondike gold fields. (Larry Pynn)

ago floating downstream on clumsy log rafts. Even ploughing upriver had its dangers. Henry Choquette, son of the famous French-Canadian miner who explored the Stikine River, was lining a stern-wheeler in 1898 when the rope snapped and crushed his leg against a wooden stump. He died of loss of blood and trauma. Although the idea was never seriously pursued, the Dominion government actually considered spending $5,000 to $10,000 to blow up the four midstream boulders that create Five Finger Rapids, effectively removing one of the major navigational obstacles on the all-Canadian Stikine Route to the Klondike.

Our canoe back in the river, we drift toward the inevitable time of reckoning, but the rapids seem to take forever to materialize. Finally, around a bend, the four boulders appear, lined up with the invincibility of football linebackers. The prevailing advice for navigating the rapids hasn't changed in a hundred years—for the safest ride, keep to the right channel. Now only seconds away from the rapids, I drop to my knees to lower the centre of gravity in the canoe and take straight aim at the left side of the right channel. We paddle hard through the choppy waters to maintain our momentum and direction, yipping and yahooing like a couple of teens on their first drunk. I can feel the waves of adrenaline pumping through my veins, swelling my confidence, and I sense the ghosts of Klondikers swirling about the eddies, cheering me on. When we emerge unscathed from the frothing cauldron, I look up instinctively at the ladder winding down the cliff from a scenic viewpoint on the Klondike Highway. Not one of the 219 steps is occupied. No one witnessed our passage through history. No one stood by to pick up the pieces in case we faltered and fell.

Just ahead to our right, the Wood Cutters Range rises magnificently to 1,200 metres from the river's edge, a symbolic welcome for those who successfully run the Five Finger Rapids. The landscape assumes a classically striking Yukon pose—mountains pinched into neat folds, topped with smooth, rounded peaks and sprinkled with golden aspen glowing ever brighter in their fall hues. A short paddle takes us to Rink Rapids, another short stretch of white water that claimed its share of paddle wheelers in its day but poses no hazard to canoeists who keep to the right side. Of far more interest to us is a thick band of white ash easily seen in the riverbank just beneath the topsoil, like a foot-deep layer of snow frozen in time. Known to some as Sam McGee's ashes (a reference to Robert Service's famous Yukon poem "The Cremation of Sam McGee"), the ashes are evidence of a massive volcanic eruption, perhaps originating in the Wrangell Mountains, around 700 A.D. Wherever it happened, the eruption has provided archaeologists with a convenient time line for dating artifacts found above or below the white band.

We make camp at Yukon Crossing, once the site of a summer ferry crossing, roadhouse and telegraph station. For years the Yukon River served as a frozen winter highway for sled-dog teams travelling between Whitehorse and Dawson. With the gold rush and increased traffic, the Whitehorse-Dawson road was built overland in 1902 to handle winter mail, shortening the distance by 160 kilometres. In the late 1930s, the road was abandoned after regular airmail service began. And by 1955, with completion of the Klondike Highway, riverboat settlements all along the Yukon River had become deserted. Sitting at our campsite near this historic site and trying to ignore the spread-shot of a woman someone has drawn on an official sign, we are amazed that such an enormously powerful river as the Yukon can be so quiet. Nothing but the occasional murmur of water passing over a boulder, or the gurgle of a whirlpool spinning off the river bottom. And overhead, the gentle whisper of wind carrying the lingering spirits of those who passed before.

Dawson resident Don Flynn, originally from Labrador, rests his beer on the partially skinned-out carcass of a bull moose, a food staple for northern residents, on the Yukon River. (Larry Pynn)

10

THE FINAL PUSH TO DAWSON

If Fort Selkirk is a museum, Danny Roberts is a museum piece. Wearing a black captain's hat heavy with souvenir pins such as "I love Vienna," he is the only native many foreign paddlers meet on their journey to Canada. "I get paid $1,000 a month to pack this book," Danny says, paging through old photographs for two German women. "They've made a lazy man out of me." Danny serves as unofficial mayor of historic Fort Selkirk. He is employed by the territorial government to collect the names of the hundreds of canoeists passing through from June to September. But those travellers who look beyond the caricature Danny has created for himself will find a native elder vibrating with history, a living relic of the Yukon riverboat days, a reminder of traditional aboriginal values before first contact with the four-wheel-drive pickup truck, the snowmobile and the all-powerful satellite dish.

Born here in 1924, Danny worked as a trapper in winter and a woodcutter for the riverboats in summer at camps up and down the Yukon River. Then one year he returned to Fort Selkirk to find

Fort Selkirk, at the confluence of the Yukon and Pelly rivers, served as a military depot for members of the Yukon Field Force after their trip up the Stikine River, overland on the Teslin Trail and down the Teslin River on hand-hewn wooden craft. (B.C. Archives and Records Service)

the stores shut and almost everyone gone. The natives had resettled on reserves at Minto and Pelly Crossing, closer to the old Whitehorse-Dawson road and the modern Klondike Highway. Only a handful remained into the early 1950s, living in tents and enjoying the traditional life of trapping, hunting and fishing. Those were the old days. When I encounter him, Danny hasn't worked his trapline for three years because of a heart condition. He would like to hand it down to his nephew, but he cannot even catch and skin a squirrel. And despite having to deal with all these crazy white people still trickling downstream, Danny prefers Fort Selkirk to his winter reserve home up the Pelly River. "It's nice and quiet," he says. "At Pelly Crossing, there's too much drinking now. People bang on the door, drunk, at two in the morning. That's how it's changed. Those kids drink and go crazy. When I was a boy living here, nobody drank."

Fort Selkirk began in 1848 as a Hudson's Bay Company post on the east side of the Yukon River near its confluence with the Pelly. It lasted only a few years before flooding forced a move to the west side, a dry, elevated terrace with a spectacular vantage over the river. The presence of the trading post infuriated the trade-conscious Chilkat Indians of the coast. They ransacked the settlement in 1852, injuring none of the whites but destroying or removing most of their furniture and provisions. After the whites left for other outposts, the natives burned the settlement to the ground, and for almost fifty years the Hudson's Bay Company did not operate in the region.

When the Yukon Field Force established its headquarters here in 1898, Fort Selkirk was proposed as the capital of the Yukon. But the soldiers didn't stay much longer than the Klondike miners. The Boer War in South Africa, combined with the abrupt departure of the American miners from the overstaked Dawson goldfields, prompted the quick withdrawal of the Field Force in 1900 for more pressing duties. After the soldiers left, traders and missionaries kept the settlement alive for years, and even the Hudson's Bay Company returned in the late 1930s for one last hurrah. But with construction of first the Alaska Highway and then the Klondike Highway, the settlement lost its sense of purpose. Indeed, if there is anything a paddle past the ghost towns of the Yukon River can teach us it is the potentially devastating impact of a highway. I am reminded of a "freedom to move" logo adopted by the British Columbia government for its highway projects a few years ago, ignoring the possibility that one person's freedom may be another's gunshot to the head.

Since Danny started packing his tourist register in 1963, he has seen the number of paddlers increase from a trickle to almost a thousand a season, most of them canoeists but also a few scatter-brains aboard wooden rafts so rickety and unwieldy the crews have to jump off when they reach Fort Selkirk. Germans form the vast majority of visitors, but the Japanese are showing an interest. "They like to travel the Yukon," Danny says of the foreigners. "Some people come back again the next year. And one guy on a kayak has travelled five times on this river." Canadians and Americans are way down the list, perhaps because North Americans have so much wilderness close at hand. One notable exception was movie star Ron Howard, who last summer canoed this way, shotgun in hand in case of bears. When one of the native workers employed restoring Fort Selkirk recognized the Hollywood actor-director from a movie magazine, he agreed to pose for photos in exchange for moose meat.

Of the many sights to be witnessed on the river, few are stranger than the young German with long, curly hair and a scruffy beard who is just now making his approach to Fort Selkirk. Paddling alone, with no concept of the J stroke, he is at the mercy of the

Danny Roberts, the unofficial mayor of the Fort Selkirk historic site, is paid to keep track of the hundreds of tourists, mostly Germans, who paddle the Yukon River each summer.
(Larry Pynn)

currents, a pathetic spider about to be flushed down the drain. When he finally washes ashore, he tells us he paid $350 for his canoe and is travelling without maps to Dawson, where he plans to buy a three-month-old husky dog, build a snow sled, and live the winter in a cabin in Alaska. "If the dog is too small, I'll put myself in front of the sled," he says matter-of-factly. Yet when he sees us spraying ourselves with mosquito repellent, he becomes a know-it-all. "That stuff is worse for you than the mosquitoes." As we walk away, Albrecht whispers that he has written the man off as "ambitious but stupid." Yet in many ways he embodies the same reckless abandon with which people left their homes and their livelihoods a century ago to chase their dreams to the Klondike.

Leaving Albrecht for a moment, I walk alone through the remnants of this once proud and thriving settlement. There is St. Francis Xavier's Church, built in 1898, the second-oldest Roman Catholic church in the Yukon. The collection plate and confessional are still intact, and the floor boards upstairs bend beneath your feet, as if to remind sinners they are treading on shaky ground. Out back is a native burial ground. One plot with blue fencing bears Tag 49: "Paul James. Died 1900." The site is deliberately separated from a little cemetery dedicated to three soldiers of the Field Force who died of sickness during their term here. The three have marble headstones surrounded by stones and chain fencing and, in the distance, peaks named after each of them—Mount Corcoran, Mount Hansen and Mount Walters. All that physically remains of the Field Force on site is an orderly room, renovated in 1984, and a depression in the ground where the other military buildings once stood.

In those days, the chasm between Indian and white was even greater than it is today. Upon his arrival at Fort Selkirk, Private Lester wrote in his diary: "I have noticed that the farther we get north the poorer the type of Indians becomes. Those in the neighbourhood for instance are very low down in the scale of humanity. They are repulsively ugly and abominably dirty. They exist largely on fish and you can smell them a hundred yards off. They seem to be an idle, shiftless lot, and never seem to trouble about making the various little fancy articles for sale or barter which we saw amongst the Indians of the Stikine and Teslin Lake." That these shiftless, low-down people had survived under unthinkably harsh conditions for thousands of years in the Yukon without the luxury of modern military provisions and hardware evidently did not carry much weight with the Field Force. You will find no mountains named after Indians here.

Proceeding down the long row of buildings bordering the riverfront, I find the Anglican competition, St. Andrew's Church, carefully restored, with a bell on a rope at the entrance. There is a schoolhouse, from which I free a small bird while admiring the folding-top wooden desks arranged beside a wood stove. The police post is a symbol of strength, displaying big log beams and a nicely reshingled roof. At the post office I release yet another sparrow from captivity before it bashes its brains out and then move on to a machine shop, a skeleton of a place that once held the entire town together. In some ways, these old cabins remind me of the castles I visited during a trip to Britain some years earlier—after a while, they all look alike. But each one inevitably holds some quirky distinction from the others—the smell, the chinking of the logs, the style of roof or subtlety of design and decor. This is Canadiana at its best. The doors of some cabins are so low you have to crouch to enter; the walls of one are lined with cardboard; another features a hand pump for water and a barrel woodstove; and in yet another the aromas from an old tin of Fort Garry coffee and a Vernon Fruit Union crate are almost palpable. Occasionally, newcomers add an unwelcome touch. In one small cabin is an inscription dated August 28, 1991: "We are Japanese. It's very, very cold."

As uniquely interesting as Fort Selkirk is, I am anxious to resume paddling down the Yukon River. There is something about the size and velocity of the Yukon that fires your imagination and sends it hurtling toward new uncharted territories. Bolstered by the fresh forces of the Pelly River, the Yukon is now swollen with speed and quiet aggression, a grey stallion galloping out of control toward the Bering Sea. The author of one of our guidebooks says he made the 275 kilometres from Fort Selkirk to Dawson in thirty-six hours. We have no intention of matching that feat, but, despite the bitter cold on the morning when we renew our journey, we are warmed by the thought that our destination is within our grasp.

Up to this point on the Yukon, Albrecht and I have contented ourselves with the sighting of one crippled moose, a couple of coyotes yelping near our campsite in the morning, and numerous birds—bald eagles eying us imperiously from treetops, a golden eagle circling for ground squirrels on a far mountain, young merganser ducks in groups of a dozen or more swimming furiously downriver ahead of us. Now the myriad of islands in this stretch are fertile habitat for black bears seeking the spawned-out salmon washed up on the gravel shoreline. At one place, we round a corner to find a huge bear standing a few metres away, staring us down. Later, we spot another swimming between two islands, but we are too late to change course and paddle up for a closer look. On another occasion, we drift silently past a bear positioned on the tip of a sandbar, its nose twitching like radar to locate us, but unable to establish a visual link.

A short distance downstream, near the Selwyn River, we meet four young German men in two canoes who'd been bathing nude in the river the night before at Fort Selkirk. Our thirty-something bodies were no match for their lithe, muscular image of youth. But in the canoe, Albrecht and I paddle with the speed and grace of killer whales at the hunt. These four young bucks are dead in the water, and they know it. "What kind of paddles do you have?" one fellow shouts as we slice confidently past them, a weak broadside salvo suggesting we must have some technological advantage.

In the early afternoon the next day, we pull ashore near Coffee Creek and shake hands with back-to-the-landers Rick and Debbie DeGraaf. A year and a half earlier they had abandoned their upper-middle-class lifestyle on the shores of Lake Superior at Copper Harbor, Michigan, and bought this forty-hectare piece of wilderness sight unseen for $35,000. "We came here for the children, not to fulfil some dream of our own," says Rick, who has been a Pentecostal minister, a horse logger (using draft horses instead of machinery to haul logs from the bush), and the owner of a manufacturing business. The DeGraafs have seven children, aged six weeks to twelve years, although you have to wonder how, given that they all sleep in the same room pending construction of an addition to their log house. "No running water, no bathtub, no toilet and all those kids," Debbie muses, touching herself up with makeup prior to being photographed. "I'm not complaining, but this is not the traditional American dream." The bone-numbing winters, the spring floods, the mosquitoes, the physical labour, the cramped quarters, and the dearth of luxuries almost sent her packing. "It's more of an adjustment for the

213

woman. I came from a beautiful home. I had a new Saab. Here everything is dirty. My horses had it better than I do now. I gave up everything I was used to—the house, the car, the material things. There were times when I wanted to call a helicopter and say, 'I'm out of here.' But the quality of life is 100 percent better here. I wouldn't go back now."

By moving to the Yukon this couple consciously weighed the risks of computer illiteracy and good-guys-finish-last naïveté against a righteous upbringing for their children in an environment free of sex, drugs and violence. "A person has seen 93,000 sexual acts on television by the age of twenty," says Rick, making me think I'm watching all the wrong channels. "How can a child really say no with all the peer pressure?" So what do the children think? Twelve-year-old Alexis laments that she has given up her friends and videos and pizzas. Yet while her new lifestyle is very busy, between home schooling and chores, she says she wouldn't trade away her newfound freedom, independence, and love for the outdoors. "I'm positive I'm going to college. But when I'm older, I'll move back here."

Out here in the wilderness where you live or die according to your own resourcefulness, there is not much call for higher education. In fact, thinking with a city mind can get you into trouble. I remember a year ago, having set forth on a 275-kilometre hike through the Northwest Territories, being assessed by a crazy old mountain man who was wearing a black garbage bag as a rain jacket and travelling with a pack of cranky dogs. After sizing me up for a few moments, the man concluded, "You've got educated sweat. Sure you've done this before?"

Until the DeGraafs clear the hurdle of Canadian immigration, they remain in the curious position of being back-to-the-landers who cannot shoot moose or catch salmon for subsistence. Instead, they buy provisions from the locals, grow their own vegetables, and pop the odd bear that gets a little too familiar. The frost-free growing period may be a short few months in this area of the Yukon, but the days are deliciously long. "Vegetables grow tremendous," Rick assures me, waltzing through neat rows of lettuce, cabbage, turnips, beets, cauliflower and carrots. "See that dirt patch there? It yielded 1,400 pounds of potatoes. They do real well in the Yukon." The garden is protected from wildlife by a solar-powered electric fence. "A moose went right through and tore the thing down the night I didn't have it turned on," he notes.

There is just one inconsistency about the DeGraafs' flight from society. By picking a homestead site on the Yukon River, the family put themselves in the path of every canoeist paddling the river. Even in the vastness of this wilderness, it would appear, you can run but you cannot hide. Rather than go against the flow and put up fences, Rick welcomes the flock to his pasture, charging five dollars a night to camp, ten dollars for bear stories, twenty dollars for true ones. He cannot turn away a friendly passerby. When a couple of paddlers ask to hang around for a while, helping with chores and the building of the addition to the house in exchange for room and board, he cannot say no. "People come a long way to see a family in the wilderness. They want to see a smiling face." Maybe he's too friendly for his own good—certainly for Debbie's, who is saddled with cooking for even more people. Tourist Andrew Glaser interrupts the manufacture of planks on a portable sawmill

Christians Rick and Debbie DeGraaf abandoned the easy life in Michigan for the hardships of homesteading on the Yukon River, a place they considered more suitable to raising their seven children, the youngest just six weeks old. (Larry Pynn)

to describe how he was fed up with his modern lifestyle in Switzerland. "I say go to Canada, build a log house, smash the TV, burn the newspapers and think about nothing. And now my dream comes up and I stay here." Officially, his flight home to Switzerland leaves from Calgary in three months, but I wouldn't be surprised if he's still roaming around the boreal forest with a chainsaw then, carving out the ultimate Swiss dream. "This is where man was made to live," he says, flicking shavings from his brow. "Probably I'll come back."

Proceeding confidently downstream in the sunshine with a copy of Rick's pamphlet, *The Steps to Peace with God* (published by the Billy Graham Evangelistic Association), I feel I am already well on the road to spiritual tranquillity. According to Rick, Dawson is only 160 kilometres away, not even a two-day paddle at the current blistering flow of the Yukon River. Toward dusk, however, we are having trouble finding a good flat campsite near a fast-flowing creek. It can be a stressful time. After so many hours of hard paddling, our last reward of the day is a dry campsite in a serene setting with a stunning view. But this evening, passing a landscape of logjams and swamps, our options are becoming depressingly limited.

Then up ahead we spot an old 7.5-metre flat wooden boat tied to a logjam. Strange: no sign of life. I shout a loud hello, knowing there is nothing more dangerous than sneaking up behind someone in the bush. A few seconds later, Ron McCready pokes his nose over the top of the logjam and invites us up. With one proviso: "No pictures until it's out of the water, okay? It doesn't look very nice." Not sure exactly what he means, but determined to find out, Albrecht and I scramble up the wedge of logs and into a wilderness twilight zone. There we find McCready, his girlfriend Diana Deren, and another couple, Lois Roscoe and Don Flynn, struggling with a block and tackle to drag two freshly shot bull moose out of a slough and onto a sand bank. It is a massacre scene. The hindquarters, hacked off to lighten the load, lie on a plastic tarp.

Blood drips from everyone's hands and clothes. "Come on," Ron encourages us. "We could use your help." For days, Albrecht and I have debated the merits of hunting and the folly of all these Europeans who come over and pay as much as US$10,000 or even more for a trophy kill—just a glorified dust collector. Now, without a second thought, we enter the fray, helping to muscle up the moose like brawny participants in a sports-day tug-of-war.

But this is no trophy hunt, folks. There is no boastful talk of the calibre of the bullet, the accuracy of the shot, or the ferocity of the beast. In fact, Don describes it as more parody than anything else. "We had the stereo going full bore—a Moody Blues tape—and we just pulled in to shore," he says, resting his beer can on the carcass. "For once, they didn't move away. They just waited for us to shoot them." For these four Dawsonites, the moose are the difference between beans and meat for the winter. "Around here, you pay eight dollars for a frozen block of hamburger," Lois says, surveying the kill with pride. "We got lucky. This will save us $1,200 worth of food."

Once the moose are out of the slough and onto the beach, Diana pulls out her knife and begins skinning and gutting the carcasses. "Ooh, that's awful," she says, turning her nose away. Albrecht, witnessing more blood and carnage here than he ever did in the Swiss army, nods in agreement. "They have a peculiar smell." To which Don replies sarcastically. "Yeah, it smells like dead moose."

Later we stand over the dead animals, their glazed eyes looking up at us, as Don fries a few strips of meat. This is like eating a hamburger at McDonald's while the cow lies sliced open next to the condiments table. "That's his back leg," Don says. "A drumstick."

The texture is lean, stringy and chewy, the taste only a bit gamy. As the beer flows, Diana whistles to draw out the northern lights, and wild-eyed Don uses gasoline to set a logjam ablaze to keep bears away. The scene takes on all the appearances of a satanic rite. "I'm a pyromaniac," shouts Don, his bushy beard and slim frame silhouetted against a backdrop of flames. "I'm one happy fucking camper. I'm gonna go roll in the sand, I feel so good."

When we leave the next morning, a cool fog hangs like dead weight over the river. We pass the shallow, braided White River, first prospected in the early 1870s and named by Robert Campbell of the Hudson's Bay Company in 1850 for the volcanic ash in the riverbank. Minutes later we reach Frisco Creek and are only too happy to accept an invitation from placer miner Sam Lenko to stop for some hot coffee, chicken noodle soup, and sandwiches. After all, today is Sam's seventy-first birthday, and we're his best bet for socializing. "Forty-nine years ago today I captured a doctor who was wounded at Reggio di Calabria," says the Second World War veteran. "He was the only Italian soldier I met who was well dressed."

Sam is likely to go off on tangents, which helps explain why a *cheechako* (tenderfoot) like himself is camping out in the Yukon in the first place. Leading us up the riverbank and into his warm cookhouse, he explains that he had worked for twenty years in the gravel business in Sangudo, Alberta, west of Edmonton. Then he figured it was time to pursue his dream—hell, pretty much every-one's dream—of striking it rich in the Klondike. Two years ear-lier, he teamed up with two partners, invested $60,000 and bought 190 quartz and placer claims. "I'm taking the profits from the

Sam Lenko made his money in the gravel business in Alberta, but now he's going for the gold, hoping to strike it rich with this wooden sluice box near Frisco Creek on the Yukon River. (Larry Pynn)

gravel company and putting it into gold," he says with a laugh. "I have invested in different things over the years and each one was a challenge. This is an adventure I think I can accomplish. I just hope I'm in the right place at the right time. I want to prove it can be done if you're determined enough despite the bureaucrats trying to screw it up."

What Lenko is referring to is efforts by the federal fisheries department to bring Klondike placer miners into the 1990s and start to reverse a century of environmental damage to fish habitat. In the Yukon today, the placer mining industry is regulated by a 114-page federal document entitled *The Yukon Fisheries Protection Authorization.* On the face of it, federal policy obliges miners to file rehabilitation plans for streambeds, including the replacing of topsoil and contouring of riverbanks to encourage faster revegetation. In addition, each stream is given a rating of one to five based on its importance to salmon and freshwater fish—arctic grayling, trout, inconnu and whitefish—and a corresponding rating for discharge of soil sediments.

Unfortunately, the document has more holes than a sourdough's socks. The authorization's title is actually an oxymoron because it is a political compromise that exempts Yukon placer miners from the fish pollution standards applied elsewhere in Canada. In a damning internal memo leaked to the press, Otto Langer, then head of fisheries habitat protection for British Columbia and the Yukon, complained that "near total immunity has been given to Yukon placer miners to harmfully alter and pollute Yukon streams." The first contentious point involves a federal Fisheries Act section prohibiting the discharge of substances harmful to fish. Elsewhere in Canada, compliance with the section is measured by the amount of sediment suspended in the water. In the Klondike, compliance is far less stringent and based on the depth of the sludge that settles in a one-litre plastic cone after one hour. The policy fails to address the fact that streams with few fish and heavy sediment may discharge directly into prime spawning streams. And the policy is toothless against placer miners who file stream rehabilitation plans and then go broke or who walk away from worthless claims leaving big messes. Finally, federal placer mining inspectors, not fisheries officers, are primarily responsible for enforcing the government's policy. These inspectors work with the industry to encourage compliance instead of rigidly enforcing the law.

The salmon that return from the Bering Sea to spawn each summer in the Klondike travel a route as daunting as those taken by the original gold seekers. After running the gauntlet of seals, killer whales, hooks and gill nets, the fish encounter placer miners as the final obstacle to a successful spawn. And a threat far more insidious than the others it is. Sediment can disorient migrating adult salmon, irritate the gills and cause disease, seep into spawning gravels and suffocate the eggs, and kill off the small plants and animals that form the base of the food chain. And yet, despite all the environmental havoc caused by placer mining, there is still something about Sam and his small operation that rekindles the romance of the gold-rush era. "I take every day as wonderful," he says. "I don't want to sit in an old folks' home. I want to keep putting one foot ahead of the other." He is the first miner we have encountered on the Yukon River. Most of the placer activity is located well up the Klondike River valley on Hunker, Bonanza, Quartz and Dominion creeks or in the Indian River valley. On this afternoon Sam's main partner, Fred Stretch, is doing some exploratory work eight kilometres upstream, leaving Sam alone as the company's PR man. "In 1973, a Montreal firm staked this country for one year. It did soil testing, but that was it. Maybe because it's a hundred miles from Dawson and hard to get in here. You need a boat. But I believe this is an untapped area." If there are proven gold reserves in the area, the partners intend to seek outside investors. "But I don't want to be like a Murray Pezim," Sam says of the flamboyant, controversial promoter on the Vancouver Stock Exchange. "We don't want any widows. Just people who can afford it. I want to give investors a return, not a bullshit deal."

Finishing up lunch, he puts on his jacket, grabs his video camera and takes us on a walk through a parklike forest of spruce en route to his placer mine about one kilometre upriver. Halfway there we stop to give him a chance to catch his breath. Here's one miner who wouldn't have made it over the Chilkoot Trail, but Lord, how he would have loved to record the view from the top with his video camera! Eventually we arrive at a hand-hewn, three-metre-long wooden sluice box. "I don't think there's another one like it in the Yukon," he says, wiping the sweat from his forehead. The placer sluice box is a simple but effective mining tool, still widely employed in the Klondike, usually on a much larger scale than this. The sluice is a trough, set at a tilt and flooded with water. River gravel is placed in the box, and as the debris washes down, the heavier gold sinks to the bottom and is trapped on a series of grooves or riffles, while the gravel passes on through with the water. So far, Sam's operation has "just scratched the surface"—the odd gold nugget and small flakes of what he calls "fly-shit gold," some platinum and a few impressive woolly mammoth tusks, relics of a prehistoric elephant that died out in the area about 10,000 years ago. "It's a challenge," he says, capturing us on video before we leave to resume our trip. "And it's a different way of life up here.

Yvonne Burian spent her childhood on Stewart Island, a former riverboat stop on the Yukon River, and is now fighting to prevent her family home from being washed away. (Larry Pynn)

Tell someone to do something here and it will take a week because they don't give a shit. Unless you look at the calendar, you lose all track of time. But at least you're out of the rat race."

Almost fifteen kilometres downstream of Frisco Creek flows the Stewart River, yet another tributary of the Yukon, North America's fourth-longest and fifth-biggest waterway. The river mouth is dominated by a battered, aging sentry: Stewart Island, the site of a former police outpost, telegraph station and trading post dating back to the 1880s, when the rich gravel bars of the Stewart River crawled with prospectors. Steam paddle wheelers also stopped here for wood, and the settlement served as a transfer point for silver-lead ore from the Mayo mine. But history didn't count for much when the Klondike Highway opened, snuffing out any reason for Stewart Island's continued existence.

Unlike so many Yukon River communities killed off by the modern highway, Stewart Island continues to generate a weak pulse. Visitors can still hear the creak of a rocking chair on a summer evening, still sip fresh lemonade on a hot afternoon. "I'll stay here for as long as I can," says Yvonne Burian, a widow patrolling her lush wilderness kingdom with crutches and a steel will. "I'd like to stay the winters too, but without someone to help me...I can hardly do anything." Born in Dawson, she came to Stewart Island at age two when her father got a job as agent for the White Pass and Yukon Railway. "I spent most of my life here," she says with a wistful look across a river that once brought business and social contact and now threatens the life she loves. "This could be the end of it."

Despite her seventy years and an arthritic back and hips, she returns each summer to visit her childhood home accompanied by a handyman willing to accept the solitude for $500 a month plus room and board. The problem is, Yvonne's world is crumbling around her. With each spring melt, the flood waters chew off a bit more of the island and threaten to undermine the entire settlement. The family home, built by the Hudson's Bay Company in 1938, has already been moved back once, and the water now passes less than a metre from the front door of the guest cabin. It's so bad you expect a helicopter news crew to show up any minute to capture on film the whole place as it washes into the river. Her only hope is to persuade the government to shore up the bank with rock to save the historic site. To that end, canoeists who come ashore either to visit her museum or because they mistakenly believe Burian's Store is still open for business (as Albrecht did, hoping for cigarettes) are asked to sign a petition. But she is the first to concede there is little government interest in the project. "Close to twenty feet fell off in the spring," she concludes. "A little piece of paradise."

As we leave Stewart Island on this September afternoon and begin our final push to Dawson, a flock of 150 or so Canada geese fly noisily overhead, not so much in perfect V-formation as resembling a string tossed to the wind. The flock is awe inspiring, but there is also something unsettling about watching geese rapidly wing southward as we paddle northward. The message is inescapable: we are completing our river journey none too soon. Winter is about to drop over the land like a big white quilt, suffocating autumn while it is still strutting its impetuous, colourful youth.

The final few kilometres of our expedition are navigated against a cold head wind and a flood of warm memories. With mounting evidence that our journey is finally over—paved highways, the

Klondike River flowing in from our right, and, almost an anticlimax, the townsite of Dawson and its colourful, offbeat collection of shacks, historic sites and touristy commercial facades, I find myself retreating once more into the past to make a final tenuous link with history.

Like the prospectors who travelled this route a century earlier, I have felt my fair share of hope and hardship, desire and disappointment. And, like so many thousands, I leave the Klondike rich, not in gold, but in experience, memories and personal insight. Moreover, I have gained an enduring respect for the people who call the North their home. Southerners might be quick to write them off as eccentric, but I have grown to envy them for having the fortitude to live where they like and say what they want. Anywhere outside the North, you could safely say that a shot-up Indian guide-outfitter, a family of Fundamentalist back-to-the-landers, and a crippled widow would have absolutely nothing in common. But along this century-old route to the goldfields, these very people are united by pride in the individual spirit, a willingness not to conform and the sense that someone must take a stand whatever the consequences. If the Klondike has a lingering legacy, it is to be found, not just in historic buildings and gold-rush relics, but in the hearts of these few resilient people. Indeed. That the spirit of the last great gold rush still burns in the imagination of Sam Lenko, a wheezing septuagenarian gravel salesman from Sangudo, Alberta, fills me with hope.

INDEX

233

Index